50+
TECH
TOOLS
FOR
SCHOOL
COUNSELORS

50+ TECH TOOLS FOR

SCHOOL COUNSELORS

HOW TO BE MORE ENGAGING, EFFICIENT, AND EFFECTIVE

ANGELA CLEVELAND
STEPHEN SHARP

Foreword by **RUSSELL A. SABELLA**

FOR INFORMATION:

Corwin
A SAGE Company
2455 Teller Road
Thousand Oaks, California 91320
(800) 233-9936
www.corwin.com

SAGE Publications Ltd.
1 Oliver's Yard
55 City Road
London EC1Y 1SP
United Kingdom

SAGE Publications India Pvt. Ltd.
B 1/I 1 Mohan Cooperative Industrial Area
Mathura Road, New Delhi 110 044
India

SAGE Publications Asia-Pacific Pte. Ltd.
18 Cross Street #10-10/11/12
China Square Central
Singapore 048423

Printed in the United States of America

ISBN 978-1-5443-3837-8

Program Director: Jessica Allan
Content Development Editor: Lucas Schleicher
Senior Editorial Assistant: Mia Rodriguez
Project Editor: Amy Schroller
Copy Editor: Deanna Noga
Typesetter: C&M Digitals (P) Ltd.
Proofreader: Lawrence W. Baker
Indexer: Molly Hall
Cover Designer: Gail Buschman
Marketing Manager: Margaret O'Connor

This book is printed on acid-free paper.

SUSTAINABLE FORESTRY INITIATIVE

Certified Chain of Custody
Promoting Sustainable Forestry
www.sfiprogram.org
SFI-01268

SFI label applies to text stock

19 20 21 22 23 10 9 8 7 6 5 4 3 2 1

CONTENTS

Part III: Organizational Tools

Part IV: Program Promotion Tools

Part V: Collaboration Tools

Part VI: Resources

FOREWORD

Technology has had a profound impact on nearly every aspect of life including education, business, religion, government, medicine, and science. School counseling is no exception. Technology cuts across everything school counselors do. From communicating to collaborating, collecting data, and understanding the responsible use of social networks, school counselors now have access to many high-tech tools. Today's online services, apps, software, and devices can help them perform at optimal levels and potentially enhance their impact on students. Maintaining appropriate technology competency is not only good for students, but it is also an ethical obligation. One challenge for us all is maintaining technological literacy while technology continues to evolve at a rapid pace. Sometimes we find ourselves trying to "keep up" with what's new, and that requires a learning curve that takes time to navigate.

At the same time, there are some apps and tools that stand out among the rest because they are user-friendly, relevant, and clearly time-savers instead of time-wasters. Finding and using tools that truly help us more effectively and efficiently fulfill our responsibilities as educators can be a thrilling experience. Yet which tools, exactly, are worth our time and attention?

I have always thought that it would be awesome to have in one place, and as a ready reference, a resource that includes the most useful technology tools for school counselors and other educators. The task, if done well, would be time-consuming and labor-intensive. Completing such a resource would require experience and insights into which tools to use and how they can help—essentially having expertise in both technology and school counseling. Indeed, this is a very tall order. In writing *50+ Tech Tools for School Counselors*, authors Angela Cleveland and Stephen Sharp have filled that order.

While there is lots of information here to digest, remember that you don't have to "get it" all at once. Technological literacy is a long-term, sustained, professional development endeavor where you practice and learn in manageable doses. Second, there is a great deal of help around you. After reading about a technology tool or tip, you can learn even more by watching online videos, asking other counselors on social networks like the ASCA Scene, and working with other educators around you who are likely to also be using the same (or similar) tools. Also, if you happen to get stuck, you can always ask one of the kids to help you figure it out. Finally, remember that, with technology, there is a very slim chance that you'll break anything, at least nothing that can't be reinstalled or fixed. So have at it! There is more than one tool here that can work for various purposes and at multiple levels. Try a couple of new tools every month for the next few months. Kick the tires; see how each one works for you.

With *50+ Tech Tools for School Counselors*, Angela and Stephen have made a valuable contribution to helping inexperienced school counselors and educators get a jump start on bringing their practice into the twenty-first century. For more experienced readers, this book will help you upgrade your technology game—get it done even better, quicker, and "wow" your students and colleagues while you're doing it!

—Russell A. Sabella, PhD
Professor, Department of Counseling
Florida Gulf Coast University
SchoolCounselor.com

ACKNOWLEDGMENTS

Corwin gratefully acknowledges the contributions of the following reviewers:

Jennifer Betters-Bubon
Associate Professor, Counselor
    Education Department
University of Wisconsin, Whitewater
Whitewater, WI

Jeffrey Gielow, PPSC MFT
Middle School Counselor
Palo Alto Unified School District
Mountain View, CA

Antanas Levinskas, PhD, NCSP
Faculty, PsyD Program in School
    Psychology
Capella University
Minneapolis, MN

Kara Proctor-Dunn
School Counselor
Lake Ridge Middle School
Woodbridge, VA

Franciene Sabens
School Counselor
Carbondale Community High School
Carbondale, IL

Diane Smith
Retired School Counselor
Smethport Area School District
Smethport, PA

Joyce Stout
School Counselor
Redondo Beach Unified School District
Redondo Beach, CA

Molly Strear
Assistant Professor in
    Counselor Education
San Francisco State University
San Francisco, CA

Shuntina Taylor
Director of School Counseling
Lake Ridge Middle School
Woodbridge, VA

Brigitte Tennis
Educator and Headmistress
Stella Schola Middle School
Redmond, WA

ABOUT THE AUTHORS

Angela Cleveland, MSEd, MEd, MA, has 15 years of experience as a professional school counselor and is a Google Certified Educator. She is an executive board member and webmaster for the New Jersey School Counselor Association (njsca.org). Angela advocates for equity and access to STEM opportunities. She is the program director for the National Center for Women & Information Technology (NCWIT) Counselors for Computing (ncwit.org/c4c).

In 2015, Angela cofounded ReigningIt (reigningit.com), a nonprofit dedicated to creating a STEM dialogue inclusive of every woman. The story-sharing platform has featured hundreds of inspiring women and K–12 influencers, and the group has provided a community of encouragement to support pathways to computer science.

Angela is a technology contributor to national publications, such as Edutopia, *CSTA Voice*, and *ASCA School Counselor*. She presents at conferences around the country to encourage the infusion of emerging careers in computer science into the school counseling profession.

Angela's advocacy has earned her recognition, such as the "2017 New Jersey State School Counselor of the Year" award and being featured in the popular Amy Poehler's Smart Girls blog.

Angela grew up in New Jersey and attended William Paterson University, where she earned degrees in English and education as well as an honors in humanities. She attended the University of Pennsylvania, earning an MSEd in psychological services. Angela began her career as school counselor in 2001, and she remained driven to learn more about the field of education and leadership. She went on to earn an MEd in instruction from the College of New Jersey and an MA in organizational leadership from Rider University. She earned several educational certifications, including Google Certified Educator, director of school counseling services, and school supervisor.

You can follow Angela Cleveland (www.AngelaCleveland.com) on

Twitter: @AngCleveland

Instagram: @angela_cleveland_reigningit

LinkedIn: linkedin.com/in/angelacleveland

Stephen Sharp is a school counselor and Apple Certified Educator. He has worked to provide students with the knowledge and skills to be healthy and successful in the twenty-first century. Stephen previously worked in his school district as a technology leader and served on the governing boards of both his local and state school counseling associations. Stephen completed his MEd at Millersville University of Pennsylvania and BA from Lycoming College.

Stephen was a contributing writer on the use of technology and career exploration in *Voices from the Field, Orientation to the Counseling Profession.*

Stephen Sharp is a cofounder of the Leadership Summit, a community-based social justice network that provides students the language and tools to understand and combat the many forms of oppression.

Stephen is a Nationally Certified School Suicide Prevention Specialist and continues to work with the Commonwealth of Pennsylvania to pilot an electronic behavioral health screening for schools. He works tirelessly across the state to provide education and training on mental health, substance abuse, inequality, and a world changed by technology.

Stephen frequently presents on technology, emerging career skills, mental health, and race in education. Stephen was named the 2017 Pennsylvania Middle School Counselor of the Year.

You can follow Steve at

Twitter: @stvsharp

Instagram: @stvsharp

GETTING STARTED

To best understand the relationship of school counselors and technology, and the course of this book, let's start with a lesson from a seasoned educator, Dr. Emmett Brown. Dr. Brown's chief role was advising a local high school student. Through advisement, Dr. Brown helped the student enrich the lives of his family members, discover his unrealized future self, explore the rich past of American history, and have the student become the best version of himself, all through the use of technology to enhance their mentoring relationship. Admittedly, the plot summary of the *Back to the Future* (Zemeckis, 1985) trilogy shouldn't be a model for school counselors and other educators regarding the use of technology. However, the principles are constant between the two. If driven to make real and lasting outcomes for those we care about, the integration of technology can be a tool to make the imagined possible.

> **Marty McFly**: What about all that talk about screwing up future events? The space-time continuum?
>
> **Dr. Emmett Brown**: Well, I figured, what the hell?
>
> (*Back to the Future*, 1985)

We stand at the edge of something remarkable, the fully realized classroom. Fresh off the lines of the First Industrial Revolution, our school systems developed, using mass-produced books and resources to educate an emerging working class. During our current industrial revolution, the Digital Age, our lives and those of our students are braided between the digital, the real, and the imagined. Through the ages, our schools remain the constant, the foundation to design the future through the instruction of our children.

> School counselors play an integral role through the context of comprehensive school counseling programs to facilitate students' acquisition of attitudes, knowledge and skills needed to achieve positive postsecondary and career outcomes. School counselors at all levels recognize that employability skills align well with ASCA's Mindsets & Behaviors for Student Success (2014). Consequently, they integrate a structure for organizing and delivering information about various careers and corresponding clusters such as The National Career Clusters Framework. (Advance CTE, 2018); (ASCA, 2018a)

The use of technology in the twenty-first century has as much to do with computers, as the twentieth-century classroom had to do with machine presses and engines. Educating in the twenty-first century, isn't simply about preparing students for work in the digital age but rather connecting with the whole student and transcending educational barriers from the past. This book serves as a guide to a range of technological resources and applications available to educators. These tools will not only enrich instruction but also do much more: gather meaningful data to guide decision making;

build positive relationships with families; enhance communication; streamline work; connect teachers to networks of innovation; and promote happier, healthier students.

Technology provides global opportunities for student learning, exploration, communication, networking and collaboration. School counselors promote the responsible use of technology in collaboration with families and educators to increase student safety. (ASCA, 2000)

LEGAL CONSIDERATIONS

Learning and sharing new technology can be hard enough without the challenge of navigating many different legal guidelines and expectations. Managing student data, ensuring student confidentiality, and providing access for all students are some of the challenges and considerations.

There are three laws to be highlighted as you begin to imagine ways to enhance your own instruction and practice.

Protection of Pupil Rights Act (PPRA)

Protection of Pupil Rights Act (PPRA) requires parent permission when conducting a screening, survey, or use of student information for marketing or sales. Permission is needed or the ability to opt out when student information includes: political or religious information; information that is mentally or psychologically embarrassing or damaging to the student or family; information about illegal or illicit behavior; information about sex attitudes, activity, or behavior; any potential critiques by the student of individuals with whom the student may have a close family relationship; income not related to access to eligibility to programs; and information about parent participation in privileged groups (lawyers, clergy, physicians, etc.).

In summary: If Clarissa is going to explain it all—in a survey or screening about something that is possibly personal or sensitive about herself or her family—you may need permission from her guardians.

Family Educational Rights and Privacy Act (FERPA)

Family Educational Rights and Privacy Act (FERPA) safeguards student records, allowing students and their parents (of students under 18 years old) access to their educational record. FERPA also has provisions to request amendments to the educational records and control of the disclosure of information of the educational record. The educational record includes directory information, attendance, discipline, schedules, class lists, financial aid information, and grades. Although guidance continues to emerge regarding FERPA and digital media, some general principles can be gathered.

- Displaying student work outside of classroom may require prior parent permission. This may include digital works in public spaces.

- Students sharing or contributing to work on third-party websites will benefit from clear expectation on online conduct and behavior and clear prompts to guide student contributions and work so as not to disclose information from their educational record.

- Teacher commentary on public digital media (like social media sites) to students directly should not reference grades or any other content of educational record. Teacher commentary in any public forums should refrain from using any information that could be from a student educational record.

If Clarissa explains it all publicly, make sure she's been coached to leave out educational record information and your reply does not share any of her information.

Children's Online Privacy Protection Act (COPPA)

Written parent permission is required prior to collecting student's personal information online (ages 13 and younger). Although directed at online services, companies, and mobile apps, school often serves as the intermediary between the two. Parents can change or rescind consent or have their child's personal information deleted. Personal information includes student name, screen name, email address, phone number, photo and/or video, social security number, geolocation, IP address, student ID, or other information that could be used to identify the student or parent.

The practical solution is to plan ahead and provide a written request to parents prior to using web technology or an application. You can get the permission either individually or in collaboration with your district's technology office, tech integrator, or instructional technology office. Continued training, education, and reinforcement with students about privacy and disclosure should also occur regularly.

If Clarissa explains it all—and is using digital or web technology that requires a login— you should get prior parent permission if she's under 13 years old.

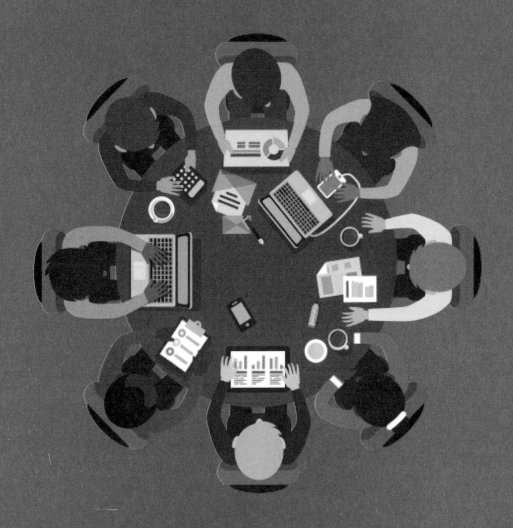

PART I

GROUPS
AND
LESSONS

NEARPOD

RECOMMENDED GRADE LEVEL	ELEMENTARY SCHOOL	MIDDLE SCHOOL	HIGH SCHOOL
LEVEL OF DIFFICULTY	EASY	MODERATE	A LITTLE MORE ADVANCED
COST	FREE	FREE TO USE PAY TO UPGRADE	FREE TRIAL PAY TO ACCESS

There are so many great digital presentation tools available today, but many are limited in that they are top-down, presenter-to-speaker tools. Active audience engagement is supported by the content the presenter adds to the slides and not via the platform.

Educators know how important it is to have engaging classroom lessons with assessment tools seamlessly built into them; they have gradually been turning to Nearpod (nearpod.com). This increasingly popular presentation tool transcends the classroom and can be used to spice up any presentation in any setting for any audience. Nearpod's motto is "Interactive lessons. Real-time assessment. Across all devices."

Nearpod has basic presentation tools, like the slides we are used to seeing and the ability to embed videos. However, this unique tool allows you to easily add real-time polls, open-ended questions, audience drawings, and more! Counselors appreciate the ability to organically collect data throughout the lesson or even at the beginning and end of a lesson by embedding Nearpod's quick survey tools and quizzes into the presentation.

As the presenter, you have the ability to see all the students' responses and pull up examples to share with the group. For example, if you want to have your students draw a circle around an example of a face expressing a certain emotion, you can have them do that and pull up a few examples to show the group. You can also add links to other websites, which is super helpful if you want to add a Google Form. For example, if a school nurse gives a presentation to staff about blood-borne pathogens, a link to a Google Form at the end of the Nearpod presentation allows staff to click and complete a survey or quiz.

It's also beneficial for participants who cannot see the screen from a distance or may need to adjust the colors and size of the presentation on their personal device to meet their individual visual needs.

Nearpod is versatile; you can present from your phone and have the audience follow along on their devices! The presenter's ability to download the app and move the slides along from a phone is a tremendous support when projection to a large screen is not an option. It's also beneficial for participants who cannot see the screen from a distance or may need to adjust the colors and size of the presentation on their personal device to meet their individual visual needs. Participation does not require a login. Another great feature is that you control the pace of the presentation. Remember the old days when you handed out a printout of your presentation? Innovative educators are sharing Nearpod links so that the group can follow along from their device. With Nearpod, YOU control the pacing and which slides appear when on the audience's devices! No more worries about people in the back of the room not being able to see small font or concerns that they are not on the right slide!

If you are just getting started with Nearpod, know that you don't have to start all over and re-create presentations you've already developed. Download the free Nearpodize This! extension from the Google Chrome store to easily convert your existing presentations! You can also check out free or low-cost Nearpod presentations by searching in Nearpod for specific topics.

Nearpod has basic presentation tools, similar to PowerPoint or Google Slides, so it feels like a familiar platform. It also has the ability to easily embed videos (something very important to me), and you can enhance presentations with real-time polls, open answer responses, audience drawings, and more!

Below is a framework for a sample lesson plan on conflict resolution geared toward sixth-grade students:

1. Open the lesson with an entertaining video hook that demonstrates what happens when two parties disagree and don't have conflict resolution skills. A good example is Dr. Seuss's "The Zax." You can find video clips on YouTube.

2. Define what conflict is, how it happens across all age groups, and how it can be resolved in many different ways.

3. Insert Nearpod Poll: With whom do you have the most conflict (parents, siblings, teachers, peers, other)? The poll helps students see that we all deal with conflict in our interactions with others. It's a great way to keep your students engaged!

4. Show a video that covers Active Listening Skills. There are many on YouTube, and you can select one that appeals to your student demographic. Insert a Nearpod quiz immediately after to review key concepts. The quiz helps you know what information to focus on. For example, I added the question: "The communication blocker 'filtering' means...."

5. Insert slides and/or videos that explain I-Messages.

6. In the drawing feature, have students circle the best examples of I-Statements for a scenario you create. Alternatively you can show a short video or give a scenario of a conflict and use the "Open-ended Answer" feature of Nearpod to have students write their own I-Statement. I like the open-ended answer because you can share out some great responses!

7. Closing: Show the Kid President video "Kid President Is Over It!" about how to disagree with people. In the "Open-ended Answer," have students write a hashtag (#) that defines what they learned about the lesson (e.g., #ActiveListeningIsKey). You can share out select hashtags as a way to review. I love using the # as a summary of student takeaways. It helps me know what aspects of my school counseling lesson resonated most with students.

Nearpod is truly one of the best presentation tools available today. It has transformed my lessons, streamlined data collection, and helped me connect with ALL my students. Nearpod is at the heart of what we care about as school counselors. We all want to have engaging, effective lessons and meaningful connections with students. And, as school counselors, we need to collect data to ensure we are meeting our goals. Nearpod supports all this in a simple, integrated platform that makes my job easier and my lessons more effective and fun!

NOTES

RECOMMENDED GRADE LEVEL	ELEMENTARY SCHOOL	MIDDLE SCHOOL	HIGH SCHOOL
LEVEL OF DIFFICULTY	EASY	MODERATE	A LITTLE MORE ADVANCED
COST	FREE	FREE TO USE PAY TO UPGRADE	FREE TRIAL PAY TO ACCESS

Many educators find StoryBoardThat to be a beneficial and engaging way to create a customized message. Rather than giving students preparation tips and a list of things to bring for state testing, school counselors are creating storyboards that describe a student getting a good night's rest, eating a healthy breakfast, and bringing the correct supplies. The entire message can be personalized to the school and student demographic.

StoryBoardThat (storyboardthat.com) can be a natural point of entry for many counselors who are new to incorporating technology into their practice. They may be using drawing activities in groups and lessons, and giving students the option to use a digital version serves to focus on the goal of the activity and not the artistic ability of the student. Many children and teens enjoy working with the digital tool over drawing because they can easily customize content and make changes. When the students used paper and pencil, changes are often reflected in smudged erasures. This is especially beneficial for students who have struggles with fine motor skills or perseverate on the perfection of drawing rather than the content.

Sample school counseling, social worker, or school psychologist activities include:

- **New Students Group**—Invite new students to a group and divide up topics to address. Topics can include managing a locker, making new friends, learning school procedures, things to do around town, and so on. Students select a topic to create a storyboard that describes a new student's experience learning about this area after you've covered it in group and they've developed experience. As a counselor, you can make copies of the storyboard, bind them together, and give other new students a little book of tips.

- **Girls' Empowerment Group**—Students make storyboards of themselves as a main character successfully managing a challenge they are facing after the counselor has addressed it in group and students have had an opportunity to practice new skills. For example, we once had a student who was developing the confidence to answer questions in class. She created a storyboard of herself using strategies to practice speaking up. Many school counselors create social stories for students using StoryBoardThat.

- **Organizational Group**—Students are referred to school counselors for organizational assistance, and school counselors know that there are many reasons why a student may struggle with organization. Some students forget to write down assignments in a planner while others may forget to bring the right supplies home to complete assignments. Some students need different supplies (e.g., accordion folder vs. binder), and others need to set aside time each week to organize supplies and clean out messy lockers or desks. Counselors are skilled at getting to the root of the problem and providing strategies to empower students. An engaging and meaningful reflective activity is for students to make a storyboard reflecting their journey from disorganization to organization based on their unique circumstances.

Get started on StoryBoardThat by setting up a free account:

1. New users are brought to a screen that walks you through setting up your first three boards, starting with a scene.

2. Users will notice that the drag-and-drop interface makes it very easy to use. After you insert the scene, you select "next." Then you select characters and other customizable options.

3. Students report that they enjoy being able to easily change the characters' skin tone, hair, and eye color, and even the colors of the characters' clothing. It's important for students to see themselves in these tech tools, and non-customizable stock characters simply cannot achieve this.

With the free account, users can make two storyboards per week of either three- or six-cell storyboards. This is the right number for most educators who are not full time in the classroom and the ideal total to use with small groups. Because there are so many ways to customize the characters, setting, and story itself, limiting students to three to six cells is still better than providing them with unlimited access. These types of liberating constraints serve to help students focus on their content.

NOTES

_____

_____

_____

_____

_____

_____

_____

_____

_____

_____

PLAYPOSIT

RECOMMENDED GRADE LEVEL	ELEMENTARY SCHOOL	MIDDLE SCHOOL	HIGH SCHOOL
LEVEL OF DIFFICULTY	EASY	MODERATE	A LITTLE MORE ADVANCED
COST	FREE	FREE TO USE PAY TO UPGRADE	FREE TRIAL PAY TO ACCESS

PlayPosit (playposit.com) is an online tool that allows users to make their videos interactive. Educators upload their videos to PlayPosit and add questions. Options include multiple choice questions, check boxes, free responses, fill in the blank, surveys, a discussion forum, and more. You can even include a reflective pause in your video and embed a link to a website. The best way to understand PlayPosit is to see what others have developed on this platform.

Get started by creating an account with your email address and a password. To get a sense of how others have made videos interactive, view some Premade Bulbs. Spend a few minutes experiencing how the interactive additions change the viewing experience from passive watching to active engagement.

PlayPosit came on the scene for me as I was transitioning between university positions. I wanted to continue the success I'd had with using a Flipped model for teaching school counseling graduate courses but it was time to consider changing up my tool of choice. PlayPosit afforded me the same opportunity to deliver key content through a narrated video format that I was familiar with, but the added advantage of PlayPosit is the ability to make the video interactive by embedding questions of various types (multiple choice, short answer, etc.) that require students to physically engage with the lecture. PlayPosit also keeps analytics in the background, too, a valuable feature if you want to have data about usage. Although there was a learning curve with PlayPosit, there is considerable potential for counselor educators or practicing school counselors who want to reach stakeholders online in a more interactive way.

—Erin Mason, PhD, counselor educator and former school counselor, Georgia State University

Educators can use PlayPosit for a variety of purposes. It's more engaging and cost-effective to create your own video-based lessons than purchase one. You can customize the content for the specific needs of students. Educators may have a set of PowerPoint or Google Slides with content they've presented. Use a screen-recording program like QuickTime Player or ScreenCastify to record your voice as you click through slides. ScreenCastify is a screencasting extension for Google Chrome, and many Google fans and Chromebook users prefer to use the extension because recordings are automatically stored in their Google Drive and it doesn't require downloading of software. The free version limits users to 10-minute recordings. QuickTime Player is also free and allows users to record longer videos. It has more editing features and must be downloaded. When the videos are uploaded to PlayPosit, the student experience is enhanced by adding interactive questions. PlayPosit allows students to learn at their own pace and answer questions and engage with others while allowing for processing time.

Educators can also record their videos from their smartphones and upload them to PlayPosit. Do you want to help new students become quickly acclimated to your school? Record a tour of your school, explain policies and procedures, share about fun events, and more! You can add questions in PlayPosit to review key areas, such as late bus times, club sign-ups, late-to-school procedures, and so on. Before students set foot in the building, they can play the videos with their family to feel more comfortable on their first day.

Have a school media specialist take a video of the tour of the library, makerspace, and more while explaining procedures for sign-up times, checking out materials, and more. Embedding questions and open-ended responses allows the educator to get feedback on the effectiveness of the video messaging and keep students engaged.

Get started on PlayPosit! Create a "bulb," which is what PlayPosit calls its interactive videos:

1. Go to PlayPosit.com, register for an account, and select "New" and "Bulb."

2. Upload your video, play it, and whenever you want to add more content, select the "+" in the menu.

3. When you are done, you can share out the link to the Bulb or you can create a class (names and email addresses) and assign the Bulb to the class.

> *Tip:* Think broadly about the term *class* to consider a class of new teachers to explain your role as a counselor as referral procedures or a class of a group of students you are meeting with about a specific topic (e.g., study skills, new student group).

PlayPosit has an option to create classes and assign the videos. This is a helpful feature for educators to use for their classes and to share information to their students, families, or staff members. Administrators have found PlayPosit to be a helpful tool to explain to teachers how to upload grades for report cards or complete other computer-based tasks. New teachers get a lot of information shared with them at orientations. Having the ability to learn at their own pace and review videos at their leisure is empowering.

PREZI

RECOMMENDED GRADE LEVEL	ELEMENTARY SCHOOL	MIDDLE SCHOOL	HIGH SCHOOL
LEVEL OF DIFFICULTY	EASY	MODERATE	A LITTLE MORE ADVANCED
COST	FREE	FREE TO USE PAY TO UPGRADE	FREE TRIAL PAY TO ACCESS

Like the Bob Ross of slide decks, Prezi is open-canvas presentation software. While traditional presentation software like PowerPoint and Google Slides shares information linearly from one talking point to the next, Prezi shows relationships between topics through a guided zoom feature, because the presentation is laid out across a large virtual poster board. Prezi takes a traditional "click and share" presentation and lays the foundation to have a deeper conversation across a wide-open canvas.

Users start by going to prezi.com, where they could create a Basic account with either an email, Facebook, or Google ID, simply by clicking on Pricing and selecting Basic. Underneath the plans you'll see "**For educators and students.**" "For educators . . ." (EDU) is the better plan for FREE. The EDU Basic Plan offers unlimited presentations, like the other Basic Plan, but also has privacy controls and share-able links.

You're ready to start a new presentation. Click on New Presentation to get started. Prezi will prompt you to pick a template. Users can scroll through the gallery or sort on the left by category or color scheme. Each template is also categorized by skill level (novice, skilled, master).

Once a template is selected, a demo can be viewed for building a prezi on the selected template. After a template is selected, users can customize and design the prezi. The background color or image can be changed by clicking on Background & Theme at the top of the screen. Each of the shapes frames a specific topic. Topic titles can be changed simply by double clicking and typing. Topics have subtopics (or subtopics can be added by clicking on Insert) that can be edited in the same way as a topic.

In addition to text, users can also click Insert at the top of the screen and add images, audio, or videos (from YouTube). Shapes can be used to add illustration or attention to the topic. Arrows can be added to guide attention or demon-strate relationship. Icons and symbols can be added for additional illustration. Animations including fading and zooming on specific topics and subtopics can emphasize important points in the presentation. Progress is synced automatically, or users can click Save along the ways. The Preview button on the top screen menu allows users to present or preview the prezi; the blue Present button launches the presentation.

When presenting, slide clicks are now replaced with a glide between talking points, zooming in and moving between topics or key points. Moving between topics and subtopics now visually reflects orientation such as proximity, tangential topics, and related works, in addition to the normal linear flow of presentation. Counselors can lead a self-discovery group for young British pop musicians and ask the Wannabes, "Tell me what you want?" and then swiftly zoom to the next topic "…is that what you really really want?" Counselors can then click and zoom into a subtopic to help explore and understand what the participants mean by "zigazig-ah."

The dashboard that holds all the presentations allows users to press Play and Present, click on the pencil to continue to edit, or click on the three dots to access sharing and privacy features. Presentations can be shared with colleagues or others to view, comment, or edit through the dashboard. A link to share the presentation can be created from the dashboard.

Prezi's open platform creates a multidimensional but conversational presentation. Complex and abstract concepts no longer need to be shown slide by slide; rather, they can be shown in relation to each other through size, proximity, or directionality by orienting Topics and Subtopics on the board. In the Information Age, Prezi transforms slides into happy little infographics, which can be infused with media-rich content to be engaging and insightful.

NOTES

FLIPGRID

RECOMMENDED GRADE LEVEL	ELEMENTARY SCHOOL	MIDDLE SCHOOL	HIGH SCHOOL
LEVEL OF DIFFICULTY	EASY	MODERATE	A LITTLE MORE ADVANCED
COST	FREE	FREE TO USE PAY TO UPGRADE	FREE TRIAL PAY TO ACCESS

As counselors and educators, one of our goals is to capture authentic student responses to drive a learning experience. Seldom does a whole class' survey responses or questionnaires reflect our students' rich and diverse thoughts and insights. Flipgrid is a video discussion forum. The underlying mechanics are similar to any other online chat group or discussion board. The facilitator has a grid; a grid is a community of learners or a classroom. Prompts are provided by the educator for each discussion topic, and then participants respond via video responses (normally 90 seconds). Each response can be viewed by all the participants and responded to by other participants, creating a platform for rich insights and discussion.

To begin, as an educator, simply go to flipgrid.com. Users can log in using your Google or Microsoft account. You can also log in using a school email address and creating a "SUPER SECRET PASSWORD" (may we suggest using the password DJTanner4Life).

Once logged in, you're ready to set up a grid. A grid is your virtual space for a community. The community can be a classroom, professional learning network (PLN), Grid Pals (a space for networking, mentoring, and discussion), Families (a space for parent engagement, updates, and providing information to a Full House), or a customized Grid. Ultimately, when setting up the Grid, think less about "What is the name of the community?" and more on "How do you want the community to engage with you, the discussions, and each other?"

Once you select a type of Grid, it will ask you to set up a Grid Password. You can select an auto-generated secure password, or customize your own (e.g., FULLHOUSE). Once a password is set up, Flipgrid will let you know Your Grid is Ready. You can click All Set in the lower right-hand corner to get started; but we prefer you click on Customize your Grid.

Customizing your Grid is an easy way to increase the accessibility and user experience. First, you can change the FlipCode from the auto-generated randomized code to something more personalized or specific like FULLHOUSE. PLCs or Public Grids can be password-protected either with a random password or a customized one (e.g., HaveMercy). The type of Grid can be changed, and here you can also preload students manually or via a CSV (comma-separated values) file. Students can also be assigned a random ID via Flipgrid.

Features such as notifications, downloads, and privacy can also be set. Finally, images can be added for a Grid Cover from either Flipgrid's bank of cover images or uploading a JPEG file thru Upload or Drag/Drop. After clicking Update Grid, you're ready to go. A Copilot can be added to monitor or facilitate a grid, as well.

Once a grid is set up, you're ready to start a discussion. A description of the grid to frame the purpose or provide guidelines or goals can be added. Flipgrid provides preformatted Topic/Discussions dependent on which grid type you've select. Here you can review or change the prompts and/or discussion questions and adjust the time for response.

Most responses are 90 seconds but can be adjusted from 15 seconds up to 5 minutes. Videos can be moderated, requiring the grid owner's approval before becoming visible, or the privacy can be set to unmoderated allowing for immediate viewing and responses. Resources to engage participants, like an emoji, GIF, or short video, can be added, as well as topic resources by simply pasting a URL and title.

Finally, video response rules can be set up. Rules for allowing responses, selfie decoration, permitting emoji responses, and the privacy level of responses are the key features in the section. Topics can be downloaded from the Disco Library (discovery library), where users can sort via audience, subject, or goal; or simply type a keyword in the search bubble. Privacy should be considered before launch. Is the discussion topic one you, as the facilitator, wish to view by yourself or spark a conversation across the community?

Here are the guiding prompts that can be provided to participants prior to starting a discussion:

1. Read the prompts or guiding questions.

2. Jot your ideas down (or even a script) using the stickies.

3. Press record (or upload a previously recorded video).

4. Hit next and review your response.

5. Take a selfie (decorations are appreciated, but not required).

6. Add information, name, or email, if so desired.

7. View submissions.

8. Reply with a video response.

The topic and/or discussion can be shared via URL, embedded into a website, or QR code. Participants only need the Flip Code and possibly a password. When logging in, participants may be prompted to enter a Flip Code. Once the participants see "Shh, this Grid is Locked," the Grid Password should be added. Participants don't need to register or download anything; they simply need a web browser and camera to participate. An app is available for iOS and Android for participants to use, if so desired. You're ready to view, moderate, and participate in these great discussions.

Counselors can use Flipgrid to supplement or modify traditional small-group or lesson content. Small groups can be flipped to spark thought-provoking discussion prior to the group sitting together or to modify existing class discussion to drive a discussion or exploration no longer dependent on a student's literacy level or native language. Sensitive topics of stress management or attitudes toward school or peers can be delivered to a whole class, with individual responses delivered privately back to the instructor. A student who would normally give single-word responses, or say "You got it, dude," may deliver deeper, thoughtful feedback through the comfort of a camera. Managing the flow of communication and interactions in a group shifts to a process of planning rather than the balancing acts of negotiation, mediation, and interpretation of member feedback.

Flipgrid captures sparks of insight and elevates student reflection in rich discourse outside the classroom. The practice lends itself to more authentic responses from our students and bridges areas in student responses such as processing, literacy, or writing. Flipgrid is a great resource for learners of all ages.

NOTES

_____

_____

_____

_____

_____

_____

_____

_____

_____

_____

_____

_____

_____

_____

_____

_____

_____

_____

_____

_____

_____

_____

STOP, BREATHE, THINK

RECOMMENDED GRADE LEVEL	ELEMENTARY SCHOOL	MIDDLE SCHOOL	HIGH SCHOOL
LEVEL OF DIFFICULTY	EASY	MODERATE	A LITTLE MORE ADVANCED
COST	FREE	FREE TO USE PAY TO UPGRADE	FREE TRIAL PAY TO ACCESS

Stop, Breathe, Think (SBT) is an app available for iOS, Android, and as a web app for FREE download. The app provides a guide to meditation and mindfulness training used to shift attention and develop focus, kindness, gratitude, and compassion. With guided meditation, self-assessment, measurement tools, and reminders, SBT is useful, helping users develop and support a mindfulness routine.

Getting started is as simple as downloading the app from the app store. Although you don't have to register to explore and sample the app and its services, registration with name, date of birth, email, and password is required to access most of the features of the free service.

Users can begin with a Check-in, "How are you?" The app guides the user to pause and survey themselves physically, mentally, and emotionally. From there, SBT will recommend several guided meditations that may be beneficial. Clicking on preselected meditation such as Joy or Gratitude allows the user to listen to soothing voices and be taken through an exploration of the concepts of the title. The guided meditations last between 1 and 15 minutes depending on the concept. After finishing, users can *favorite* or *share* the meditation, check in to monitor emotional or mental change, view their progress, or pick another track. Completion of meditation earns users stickers to celebrate the gains and milestones as they grow their mindfulness practice.

If the user clicks the Explore button, they can now access the extensive library of meditations. Breathing exercises, yoga, and mindfulness walking can be viewed. Users can also view the premium features, which are locked. Premium has a fee but offers exclusive and extended content for meditation.

Users can also check out the Feed, a chatbot that provides motivation and shares new content to engage the user. The content can include the Practice of the Day, motivational posters, and setup for reminders and prompts. Users can monitor their Progress (from the number of days of successive meditation *streaks*), track Settledness (the progress of inventoried emotions), view the top emotions identified, and see which meditations are the favorite.

Basic guides on how to meditate and information on the basic impacts of meditation in the brain are also available in the app in the More section. Additional information on beginning and maintaining a mindfulness practice can also be found in More. The app can be synched with the Apple Health app to provide more feedback on the gains made through mindfulness and notifications to continue with the practice.

SBT is an accessible entry into building and maintaining a mindfulness practice. The content is both warm and engaging, with a library that doesn't seem repetitive. The library is extensive enough that there's a satisfying user experience without paid content.

The content is so good there's even a children's app.

Stop, Breathe, Think Kids

Stop, Breathe, Think (SBT) Kids is the kids' version of the popular mindfulness app for adults. The velvet smooth-voiced guided meditation of the adult app is traded out for thoughtful and engaging children's videos to guide young children through age-appropriate meditation and brain breaks. The app is available for iOS or as a web app at kidsapp.stopbreathethink.com.

After download or when accessing the web app, users will be asked to immediately register. An email is all that is require. An email will be sent containing a PIN. The PIN will be used to register and then create an eight-character password. Up to five kids can be added to the account. Once names have been added, you're ready to begin; click Start in the lower right-hand corner.

Starting with Find a Mission will have children Check-in, reflecting on their emotions using a series of emojis. Missions replace the adult meditations. Each emoji reveals up to four corresponding emotions for a child to select. Once up to three emotions have been selected, users can click Launch in the lower right-hand corner.

A soft voice narrates brief stories and meditations to accompanying animation. Children will be asked to shift attention, explore emotions, or focus their breathing. After completion of the 2- to 6-minute videos, young meditators (or their adult helpers) click Complete and are asked to reassess up to three emotions again. Kids are rewarded with stickers, similar to the adult version. Children can continue with additional missions or return to the home screen.

Like the cough-syrup bottle of apps, the Settings for the SBT Kids are virtually child-proof on the app and cannot be easily changed due to the unique security feature: MULTIPLICATION TABLES. The secured adult features include background information on the app and its content.

The library of material is limited to about two dozen videos, with additional videos available for purchase as premium content. The fee for a single SBT Kids annual subscription is approximately the same as the fee for both adult and kids services combined.

Counselors can use the app to provide an introduction to these essential skills in attention, focus, and regulation. The data and scaling can provide excellent insights to monitor progress and guide feedback. The app can be great to start or complement instruction for a mindfulness practice.

Like the adult version, Stop, Breathe, Think Kids is an easy and accessible guide to develop a mindfulness practice. Adult set-up is necessary, and children should collaborate with adults for their first few missions. The missions are inviting and thoughtful and can provide children with valuable lifelong skills.

Other mindfulness apps for kids include:

- Breathe, Think, Do Sesame
- CALM
- DreamyKid
- Kids Yoga Deck
- Mindful Powers
- Mind Yeti
- Smiling Mind

Sesame Street has created an app (available in both English and Spanish) called "Breathe" where they state, "Little Children, Big Challenges." The app targets preschool-aged children and gives them real-life scenarios where they may find themselves feeling frustrated. Children learn the value of "belly breaths" to feel more calm, and how to think of a plan to solve the presenting problem. The app is beneficial as it takes children through the calming and problem-solving steps in a fun and developmentally appropriate manner. Children as young as 3 have repeated the steps, "Breathe, think, and do" to use in times of frustration.

—Vanessa De Jesus Guzman, MA, LAC, NCC, is a middle school counselor and licensed therapist with 15 years' experience working with children ages 3 to 13.

HEADSPACE

RECOMMENDED GRADE LEVEL	ELEMENTARY SCHOOL	MIDDLE SCHOOL	HIGH SCHOOL
LEVEL OF DIFFICULTY	EASY	MODERATE	A LITTLE MORE ADVANCED
COST	FREE	FREE TO USE PAY TO UPGRADE	FREE TRIAL PAY TO ACCESS

Timeless, one of the earliest incarnations and standards of the mindfulness app genre, and distinctly British, Headspace is the Doctor Who of meditation apps. The fan base for Headspace in the world of mindfulness and meditation is comparable to the following of Time Lords in science fiction. The storied beginnings of Headspace find a former Buddhist monk leaving the Tibetan monastery to share fruits of meditation with the world. Fortunately, guided meditation is significantly easier to learn and understand than the history of a BBC television show.

The Headspace app is available for download for either iOS or Android platform or can be accessed by using the web app at www.headspace.com. Getting started is easy with an email address, Facebook, or Spotify account. The app will ask your level of experience from None to A Little to A Lot, with the amount of prior experience changing the duration of the initial meditation times. To customize the experience, Headspace asks about why you're using the app: to improve sleep, ease anxiety, manage stress, find calm, and other experiences. The app will then try to find the best time to build a mindfulness routine.

You're ready to get started! There's a nice introductory video discussing the basics to meditation and building a routine, "getting some headspace." The app is intended to help build a 10-day mindfulness routine and learn the basics of meditation.

The guided meditations are narrated by TED Talks MVP Andy Puddicombe, who lulls users in mindful engagement with the warmth of English charm. Although geared for a 10-day practice, the allure of the British accent makes each session seem more timeless than trips through time and space on a TARDIS.

The educational videos are fun, complemented by humorous animation. Each of the animations serves as great educational tools and illustration to the concepts. Users can explore more of the animation through the animation library. In addition to the 10-day routine, there are other concepts of wellness and mindfulness that can be explored through Discover. This is where the application becomes more limited. The quality of each guided meditation is very good and consistent, but outside the initial 10-day basics, the library is limited and requires a subscription to access most content. Subscriptions are available for a fee and include additional packs, other guided meditations themes, minis (short meditations), meditations for kids, and the rest of the animation library.

Under the Profile menu, users can view their stats and review previous meditations under My Journey. Friends and companions can be invited to join via email under Buddies. Users can also manage their privacy and notifications under Setting found in the Profile section and receive feedback on common obstacles for both meditations practice and technical support.

Headspace is a great way to begin a mindfulness practice. The app is both informative and engaging. The app seems difficult to support an ongoing practice without a financial investment from the user, but the investment may be beneficial if the user has a strong response to the app and its services while learning mindfulness.

NOTES

_____

_____

_____

_____

_____

_____

_____

_____

_____

_____

_____

_____

_____

_____

_____

_____

_____

_____

_____

_____

_____

_____

_____

_____

INSIGHT TIMER

RECOMMENDED GRADE LEVEL	ELEMENTARY SCHOOL	MIDDLE SCHOOL	HIGH SCHOOL
LEVEL OF DIFFICULTY	EASY	MODERATE	A LITTLE MORE ADVANCED
COST	FREE	FREE TO USE PAY TO UPGRADE	FREE TRIAL PAY TO ACCESS

Insight Timer is a popular meditation app available on iOS and Android devices. It is also available as a web app at insighttimer.com. The app states they offer the "largest free library of meditations on earth." The immense and diverse content includes guided meditations, ambient noise, music, lectures, and spoken word.

New users can log in with an email or Facebook account. Insight Timer will ask your experience with meditation, to better customize the experience. The app feels like a social media experience through the lens of meditation. The home menu Today provides a feed of all the recent activity across the platform. Users can enter a location under Nearby to see who is using the app locally, and friends can be added by typing in a specific user's name or email (friends are not automatically added from a Facebook registration).

The platform touts over 10,000 meditations and a growing library. The meditations are grouped by categories: meditations, music, popular, teachers, talks, and playlists. Each meditation is also tagged, so themes, styles, and topics can be sorted and searched for easily. There are playlists for users to be guided through several meditations. Users can also participate in discussion groups to further explore topics and connect or support each other as they develop a mindfulness practice.

There is also the central feature and namesake of the app: the timer. The timer lets users meditate for a set period time to the tones of Tibetan meditation bowls or ambient noise. Users can customize the timer's duration and tones and save them as Presets.

Although most of Insight Timer's contents are free, users can purchase Courses. Courses are a series of talks, guided meditations, or instructional lessons that can be purchased for a single use at a lesser fee or unlimited use at a higher cost. By clicking Profile, users can adjust privacy settings, contact support, connect to Apple Health, and/or monitor their stats and progress.

There is a rise in the number of online meditation services available with most costing a fee for expanded content. Insight Timer stands out with the sheer volume of free content. Counselors should have no problem finding a meditation for themselves or to complement a group or activity. The app's vibrant social experiences also make the platform feel like the most connected of the mindfulness apps available. The connectedness not only promotes engagement but also is one of the most compelling tools to begin and maintain a mindfulness practice.

NOTES

_____
_____
_____
_____
_____
_____
_____
_____
_____
_____
_____
_____
_____
_____
_____
_____
_____
_____
_____
_____
_____
_____
_____

QUIVERVISION

RECOMMENDED GRADE LEVEL	ELEMENTARY SCHOOL	MIDDLE SCHOOL	HIGH SCHOOL
LEVEL OF DIFFICULTY	EASY	MODERATE	A LITTLE MORE ADVANCED
COST	FREE	FREE TO USE PAY TO UPGRADE	FREE TRIAL PAY TO ACCESS

One of the most in-demand topics in school counseling is stress management. School counselors and other educators are incorporating relaxing coloring into groups and classroom activities. This low-cost, easy activity is a soothing, creative outlet, and it provides stress relief when feeling overwhelmed. When coloring, our mind drifts off, and it provides a space for free-thinking and problem solving. Sometimes when distracted by something soothing, our best ideas come to us. You've likely had this experience when taking a walk, driving, or taking a shower.

QuiverVision takes coloring to the next level! Download their free coloring pages at quivervision.com. Our favorites are the dragonflies and airplane. Both are free.

Print out the pages, color them in, and use the free QuiverVision app (available in iOS and Android) to scan the page. The effect is eye-popping! Suddenly the image comes off the page in 3-D and comes to life in augmented reality!

QuiverVision provides me with an opportunity to talk to students about the intersection of areas of interest with advances in technology and make connections to career opportunities in computer science.

—Bobbi-Jo Wathen, school counselor in Connecticut

School counselors, teachers, social workers, and school psychologists are using QuiverVision to address several topics:

- *Stress/Worries*—Educators use several strategies to address student worries and stressors. Muscle relaxation, deep breathing, and more are enhanced for students on the highway to the danger zone of behavioral outbursts when educators incorporate the airplane in QuiverVision. Students draw their fear or frustration on the banner to help visualize stressors flying away.

- *Waiting in the Office*—Leave the Dragonflies coloring page in the main office along with a box of crayons. Students who have been sent out of class for misbehavior are encouraged by the office staff to color the pages. This helps reduce the students' stress levels. It also provides a relaxing activity for students rather than having them sit and ruminate on frustrations or cause further disruptions. The administrator or counselor can then approach a much calmer student and show how what he or she colored can be brought to life using the QuiverVision app. This leads to discussions about other applications for augmented reality and sparks interest in technology. School nurses also use these for students who may be in their office due to stress.

Check out QuiverVision's Pinterest page to see how school counselors and other educators are using this AR Tech tool: pinterest.com/QuiverVision.

COSPACES

RECOMMENDED GRADE LEVEL	ELEMENTARY SCHOOL	MIDDLE SCHOOL	HIGH SCHOOL
LEVEL OF DIFFICULTY	EASY	MODERATE	**A LITTLE MORE ADVANCED**
COST	FREE	**FREE TO USE PAY TO UPGRADE**	FREE TRIAL PAY TO ACCESS

CoSpaces (cospaces.io) is an innovative, intuitive technology tool that provides educators and students with a platform to create their own augmented (AR) or virtual reality (VR) spaces. Rather than being users of AR and VR, be a creator in a platform educators are adopting as a digital project-based learning platform.

Educators want to empower their students to view technology through the lens of problem solving and a platform for creativity while fostering collaboration during classroom lessons and other activities. CoSpaces is a trusted platform to achieve these goals while teaching real-world skills!

CoSpaces EDU (cospaces.io/edu) is an incredible, transformative ed tech tool that allows the user to move beyond consuming content to actually creating virtual and augmented reality worlds limited only by the user's vast imagination. The tool itself is fairly easy to use after taking time to explore, which allows the user to get both acquainted and acclimated to its features.

—Andrea Trudeau, MSEd, NBCT (@Andrea_Trudeau) is a self-proclaimed "no shh librarian" at Alan B. Shepard Middle School in Deerfield, Illinois, who enjoys working each day in a learning commons that emphasizes innovation, creativity, kindness, community, and, most important, fun for all.

CoSpaces allows users to create a virtual environment to be viewed and experienced using a VR headset (such as Google Cardboard, which can be purchased for around

$15) or to explore a space with a tablet or computer. Unlike other VR and AR content that requires a viewing device, CoSpaces offers more flexibility in viewing options.

CoSpaces can be used to highlight strategies to solve real-world problems: School counselors address learning strategies, self-management skills, and social skills as defined in the American School Counselor Association's *Mindsets and Behaviors* (2014). For example, "B-SMS 7. Demonstrate effective coping skills when faced with a problem." CoSpaces provides the ideal platform for counselors to create scenarios based on common problems students in their caseload present with. No longer are counselors tied to generic problems, but they can create content that is personalized for their students' demographic and needs.

For example, school counselors can use CoSpaces to create customized scenarios.

To address conflict resolution using CoSpaces, upload a 360-degree photo of your school's playground. Insert child characters having a conflict about a game of four-square. Next, create open-ended questions about how to resolve conflicts from the perspective of different characters.

Counselors integrate lessons about careers at every grade level. American School Counselor Association's (ASCA) *Career Conversation Starters* (n.d.a) (available for several age groups in English and Spanish) offers career conversation prompts that any educator can access and use.

For example, educators might offer a selection of prompts for students to develop a CoSpace such as:

1. What world and/or community challenges do you want to solve?

2. How would you approach this challenge differently than what is being done in the world and/or your community now?

3. Can you think of careers related to tackling this challenge?

4. Can you think of any STEM careers related to tackling this challenge?

> *Tip:* Find more prompts at ASCA's *High School Career Conversation Starters* (n.d.b).

To get started, visit the Welcome to CoSpaces EDU space at cospac.es/K0ea.

1. Start on your first space by selecting Create Space and then select an environment.

2. The bottom menu allows you to add content, such as people, plants, and pets.

3. You can add animation to objects and adjust their size in the environment.

4. Add text bubbles and more to customize your space.

5. You can share your space easily with a link or QR code. The sharing feature is a great way to create an engaging virtual gallery walk.

> *Tip:* The best way to understand CoSpaces is to explore other peoples' spaces! Doing so gives you a sense of the versatility of the platform and the creativity of users, and it will inspire you to get started.

> *Tip:* You can also view video tutorials on CoSpace's YouTube Channel and join the CoSpaces Edu Community on Facebook to connect with other educators.

CoSpaces is an appealing platform for school counselors employed in virtual schools. Learn more about the ASCA (2017b) guidelines in the position statement titled *The School Counselor and Virtual School Counseling.*

Users can view spaces on their computers and experience interactive components. If users pull up the space on their smartphone, it can be viewed in VR with the use of a headset. Users who don't have access to a headset are not limited in their ability to learn from the content.

Visit the CoSpaces EDU Forum (forum.edu.cospaces.io) to connect with other educators, get ideas, and get answers to all your questions from educators using CoSpaces. You can also follow CoSpaces EDU on Twitter at @cospaces_edu and follow key hashtags such as #CoSpacesEdu and the Twitter Chat #ARVRinEDU.

NOTES

_____

_____

_____

_____

_____

_____

_____

_____

_____

_____

_____

GOOGLE EXPEDITIONS

RECOMMENDED GRADE LEVEL	ELEMENTARY SCHOOL	MIDDLE SCHOOL	HIGH SCHOOL
LEVEL OF DIFFICULTY	EASY	MODERATE	A LITTLE MORE ADVANCED
COST	FREE	FREE TO USE PAY TO UPGRADE	FREE TRIAL PAY TO ACCESS

Google Expeditions is an immersive and collaborative virtual reality (VR) experience. Through cell phones, users either manage or participate in a multitude of prese-lected expeditions. As school counselors, we have access to captivating tours of colleges and career experiences with only a few clicks and swipes. Google Expeditions can transport students to campuses across various regions, sizes, and settings. A student need only begin with a cell phone, because the Google Expeditions app is free. Students can toggle between VR goggles or full screen mode. On a cell phone or tablet, counselors take the lead, selecting an expedition, and after selecting the appropriate campus, need only wait for the students to click to join.

Here is an example: For the tour, select Penn State: Main Campus. Press Play and begin in the lobby of Old Main. The polished redbrick shines, as do the glowing white pillars. As students explore the centuries-old building, the counselor guides them through prepared questions and talking points provided to them through the app. As a guide, the counselor can share details on a mural by Henry Varnum Poor and other features of the building including portraits and the foyer. The participants are led to each feature by a white arrow that appears on their screen.

Swipe right, press play, and the group is transported to Hetzel Union Building, surrounded by collegians eating and studying (and one welcoming a mascot in the distance). Touching the drawing icon at the top of the screen, the counselor can circle the Nittany Lion so everyone can see the character waving in the crowd.

The next swipe and the group is outside on The Mall surrounded by trees, buildings, and students in shorts, followed by a visit to the campus creamery where fresh ice cream is served. With two swipes the group breezes through the Meteorology Department and lands at the Nittany Lion Shrine. After a visit with the limestone mountain lion, the counselor can virtually use the group to enter the College of Education's Krause Innovation Studio: The futuristic setting is a chance to explore with the students a vision of a collaborative and creative educational experience for them now and in the future. There's a brief stop at the picturesque Arboretum before entering the Library.

Finally, the group lands on the 50-yard line of Beaver Stadium. Students can turn and are surrounded by a stadium with a capacity of more than 100,000. On a Saturday after-noon on ESPN, they wouldn't be able to explore the stadium in such a personal manner.

After about 30 to 45 minutes, any counselor can take his or her students through Pennsylvania's largest public institution without a bus, permission slips, or need for chaperones. What comes next is a truly powerful experience: They can then explore

Stevens Institute of Technology, Bowdoin College, or Howard Community College. Constraints of finance, readiness, and transportation are swiped away with Google Expeditions or other campus VR tours like YouVisit. The whole experience becomes a grand introduction to postsecondary preparedness.

Other steps to build a virtual postsecondary tour experience could include:

- Start with a pretest for this activity. It's great way to capture students' early understanding of college and the amount of growth that follows.

- Provide a brief lesson on postsecondary options, basic vocabulary, and big ideas including types, size, cost, aid, and admissions.

- After a brief discussion of the devices, app, and joining process, explore institutions across the United States while in the confines of a classroom.

- A whole group discussion lets the students share their experiences. There is normally a lot of energy and excitement after such an engaging experience. We dialogue about the aspects and type of campus, its perceived benefits, and an imagined future.

- A traditional posttest captures the student experience and any change in knowledge of college or shift in attitudes, including postsecondary aspiration. Using their devices, students could also do another reflective piece such as a video-log like Flipgrid (page 16) or Padlet (page 88) discussion.

Many outcomes are associated with this captivating VR experience. For example, a class can be introduced to the college search process, or a single student can imagine his or her college life while taking a self-guided tour on a smartphone.

Google Expeditions not only opens the doors to distant campuses but also exposes students to careers. Nontraditional, STEM, and adventurous occupations can be experienced as easily as a virtual stroll through a college park. Complex issues such as immigration or the vestiges of slavery can be explored with real, tangible interactions. Google Expeditions is realized education, where immersive and engaging experiences can be shared that transcend the confines that surround many of our students. Explore the app. Walk virtually through historic buildings, dabble in jobs you never thought you'd try, and be guided through difficult stories of our nation's past. Once comfortable, pack up your students and take them along with you using this futuristic technology.

Many students of color, first-generation and low-income students aspire to college; however, the college application process can present significant obstacles (Page & Scott, 2016). Some students in schools report there is no adult in the school with whom they feel they can discuss these issues, and many of these students come from underrepresented social or cultural groups. These students cannot always rely on their parents for college information and must instead turn to their high schools, where school counselors are in a position proven to increase access for students. School counselors can also play a role in assisting students in identity development contributing to their success (Maxwell & Henriksen, 2012). (ASCA, 2006)

GONOODLE

RECOMMENDED GRADE LEVEL	ELEMENTARY SCHOOL	MIDDLE SCHOOL	HIGH SCHOOL
LEVEL OF DIFFICULTY	EASY	MODERATE	A LITTLE MORE ADVANCED
COST	FREE	FREE TO USE PAY TO UPGRADE	FREE TRIAL PAY TO ACCESS

GoNoodle (gonoodle.com) is a website and smartphone app with a compilation of interactive videos encouraging movement and mindfulness for kids in elementary grades. It is much like YouTube Kids, except each video is designed by GoNoodle to keep students engaged and excited about each movement activity. You can search different themes and lengths of activities (1–15 minutes). Each video in a theme is under 2 minutes long, designed to keep the students interested in the research-based movement. New videos are constantly being added to keep up with current events and engage your students in fun brain and body breaks!

GoNoodle requires an internet-accessible computer with a large screen, a smart TV, or some other way to project. Speakers or the ability to play the music at a higher volume will help engage your students.

Get started by creating an account with minimal information and immediately get access to millions of themed activities and videos:

1. The Discover tab shares the newest videos and favorites among all GoNoodlers.

2. Select the Categories tab to search for the perfect video that aligns with your curriculum or activity. There are activity themes for
   - Mindfulness topics (i.e., build empathy, compassion, or boost confidence);
   - Engaging different sensory and motor skills;
   - Specific movement types like stretching, dancing, or a *brainercise*; and
   - School day transitions—this may be particularly useful on a day that has a unique schedule for students who like to stick to a routine; like the "Lunch—Blazer Fresh" guided dance video.

> *Tip:* GoNoodle transition videos are great for adults, too! The "Lunch—Blazer Fresh" video is a fun transition to lunch in a full-day workshop, and the "Melting—Flow" video is great for a faculty meeting or to share out with staff and students after a big day like state testing.

3. You can find out more information about the video by selecting the *i* when rolling your mouse over the clip. Favorite the video by clicking the heart, and identify the main movement category listed under the title of the video.

4. GoNoodle has multiple character groups with storylines that students from all backgrounds can relate to. Find videos with those specific characters under Channels.

5. Videos that you favorite can be found under the Heart tab on the menu bar.

> GoNoodle is a digital, regulation tool for schools and beyond. Teachers and counselors know best what their students' energy levels, emotional states or attention needs are at any given moment. Meeting students where they are and then taking them where they want them to go is an invaluable ability for every teacher and counselor. Predictable and fun movement, motivating sing-a-longs and re-focusing mindful practices, led by familiar characters, can be just what an over-energized, drowsy or distracted bunch of elementary students needs to re-regulate and get back to learning.
>
> —Wynne Kinder MEd, the concept/script writer of GoNoodle's FLOW, Think About It, Maximo and Blazer Fresh SEL channels.

School counselors use GoNoodle to teach self-management skills. The section on mindfulness addresses many counseling themes. Both experienced and novice counselors benefit from viewing the videos and learning new strategies to address topics. For example, many counselors have taught progressive muscle relaxation, but visuals in the Melting video provide a new metaphor for counselors to turn to. Also, playing the video and working on the activity with students rather than leading them allows the counselors to focus on the experience of students rather than their role leading.

Another fantastic video counselors use is "Relieve Anxiety" found in GoNoodle Empower Tools activity. It's possible to make a hands-on video-based activity as the speaker in the video demonstrates the use of a Hoberman Sphere, a common counseling tool to teach deep breathing.

GoNoodle offers a program for schools to sign up through GoNoodle Plus for Schools. Simply enter your school's information, and administration will be notified of the request. Signing up for a GoNoodle Plus for Schools can give GoNoodle access to all teachers and staff in a single school or entire school district.

Parent and Kid accounts are also available for free through GoNoodle. Inform families of the benefits of GoNoodle to encourage physical and mental health at home. Families will love the short educational videos that get their kids off the couch and releasing some energy!

NOTES

_____

_____

_____

MINECRAFT

RECOMMENDED GRADE LEVEL	ELEMENTARY SCHOOL	MIDDLE SCHOOL	HIGH SCHOOL
LEVEL OF DIFFICULTY	EASY	MODERATE	A LITTLE MORE ADVANCED
COST	FREE	FREE TO USE PAY TO UPGRADE	FREE TRIAL PAY TO ACCESS

Minecraft can be a tool to platform lessons on design, collaboration, and communication. More complex concepts like circuits, programming, chemistry, oceanography, and conservation can also be taught. Skilled educators focused on setting goals with the students and driving the learning through both support and inquiry can stage Minecraft to be a key component in project-based learning.

Minecraft is *the* open world sandbox collaborative building video game. At its base, Minecraft is simply a game; one with few defined objectives and no clear narrative. Players navigate through the open world digging blocks and constructing structures with blocks, while fighting monsters. At the heights of Minecraft, the game is a near endless world of creation and possibility, able to harness a wide range of computational and social emotional skills through gameplay. Minecraft is a game developed by Mojang and owned by Microsoft.

Players assume the role of avatars that can be partially customized through the selection of different "skins" or player designs. Players move throughout the world using the keyboard's W A S D buttons to move forward/back/left/right and mouse/trackpad to look around and select objects, or through a directional pad on the screen and touchscreen features on mobile devices (pocket edition). Players can use specialized tools such as shovels and axes to perform specific tasks like digging and chopping. There is a wide range of tools and items for players to collect and use throughout the game.

There are two primary game modes: Survival—players, through collecting resources, build structures and manage their hunger all while occasionally taming or fighting mobs (non-playable characters are often animals or monsters); Creative—where invincible players can fly through the endless world and have a limitless inventory of almost all blocks and items to build, explore, and design. Users are able to play by themselves, on a local area network (everyone is connected to the same Wi-Fi network), or online through servers. Users can also purchase realms, a subscription-based server system through Mojang that provides a range of mini-games, adventures, and customized worlds.

Minecraft is the only fee-based service highlighted in the book. The game's level of engagement, how deeply connected the service already is in students' lives, and emerging prevalence in education made the game feel like a necessary addition. The game is available across nearly all electronic and video game playing devices. The desktop and laptop version ("Minecraft Java Edition") has a FREE demo for download, but the actual game costs about the same as a standard PC game. Mobile device cost is significantly cheaper and can be used across devices with the same login and operating system ("Pocket Edition" or "PE"). The video game console edition costs vary, depending on the console and seller.

Separate is Minecraft Education Edition. Minecraft Education Edition has the ability to set up classrooms, allowing students to interact and work collaboratively in a classroom up to 30 students. Teachers can monitor and manage players, interactions, and world settings. Additional blocks and features are provided in the Education Edition to help guide players and gameplay. Minecraft Education Edition provides everyone in the classroom with an account, at a cost per user through a district licensing agreement available through a district's Microsoft Education Partner. Free licenses are also available to trial to game and service. The service also provides a range of supports for educators like tutorials, mentors, trainings, and lesson plans.

Once a regular membership is purchased, the game can be downloaded from the site www.minecraft.net. Once you've entered the email address and password provided during registration at time of purchase, you're ready to play. Minecraft Pocket Edition can simply begin by downloading the game and pressing play.

Minecraft can be a tool to platform lessons on design, collaboration, and communication. More complex concepts like circuits, programming, chemistry, oceanography, and conservation can also be taught. Skilled educators focused on setting goals with the students and driving the learning through both support and inquiry can stage Minecraft to be a key component in project-based learning. The engaging and immersive atmosphere can foster student voice as they explore and make decisions. Counselors can have students have collaborative tasks of building and use the activity to illustrate and foster rich discussion on soft-skills. There is a wealth of resources for educator training including webinars, mentoring, and lesson plans at the Minecraft: Education Edition Homepage, education.minecraft.net.

Ultimately, the learning experience with Minecraft can be endless and begin with a simple prompt like "build a house."

NOTES

PART II

DATA COLLECTION TOOLS

KAHOOT!

RECOMMENDED GRADE LEVEL	ELEMENTARY SCHOOL	MIDDLE SCHOOL	HIGH SCHOOL
LEVEL OF DIFFICULTY	EASY	MODERATE	A LITTLE MORE ADVANCED
COST	FREE	FREE TO USE PAY TO UPGRADE	FREE TRIAL PAY TO ACCESS

Alex, I'll take "Free web-based platforms that gamify assessment for ages 5 to 100." Hmmm, every answer is "What is Kahoot!?"

Kahoot! (kahoot.com) is a great way to share fun quizzes with a group of people from little kids to adult kids! The platform is completely free, and participants can use a computer, tablet, or smartphone. Participants don't need to create an account to participate. They simply go to kahoot.com, select play, type in the game PIN, and go!

Teachers have been using Kahoot! as a review for assessments. School counselors are using it to introduce themselves and school services to students, as a formative assessment tool in large group lessons, and with families and staff to quickly and easily gain a snapshot of what the target audience recalls. It's also a great tool to collect data seamlessly and to engage a large participant pool. School counselors recognize the value of using data as an advocacy tool, and gamifying data collection ensures that counselors can capture the voice of every student.

> Becoming proficient at using data will help school counselors efficiently serve their students and have intentional guidance or counseling services. (ASCA, 1988)

At the start of the school year, school counselors make the rounds to classrooms to talk about school counseling services and introduce themselves to students. However, students are inundated with a lot of information, and counselors want to ensure they focus on topics students may not know much about. They also want to ensure students have a positive first experience with the counselor.

Go to kahoot.com and search "School Counselor," "Get To Know Your Teacher," "Student Selfie," or "What You Did This Summer" to find ways that lots of school counselors and other educators have made to introduce themselves, get to know students, and turn Kahoot! into an engaging icebreaker. You'll see questions about the role of the counselor, how to make an appointment, school policy, navigating a locker, and more.

> Gamifying the dissemination of this information ensures participation and helps counselors know what topics to cover with more depth based on responses.

These are typically not topics that energize children, but they are important to cover. Gamifying the dissemination of school procedures and policies ensures participation and helps counselors know what topics to cover with more depth based on responses. For example, you might include a question about procedures when arriving late to school. If you notice that most or all students gave correct answers, you don't need to elaborate too much on the topic. However, if you notice that most or all students gave an incorrect response, you know this is a topic to spend more time on. Kahoot! gives counselors the opportunity to immediately customize information they share in depth based on real-time information from students.

Students love Kahoot! as a fun review of a classroom lesson, but educators love the rich data collection tools. School counselors include a quick 5- to 10-question kahoot quiz at the end of their lessons to drive home key points and also to collect data about which topics didn't resonate with students. Kahoot! allows you to download a spreadsheet that provides a summary of participant responses and a question-by-question breakdown of responses. Counselors use this data to assess effectiveness of the lessons and also to look for themes in responses. If a counselor notices that most students are still struggling to identify what an I-Message is, the lesson can be tweaked to ensure this topic is covered more clearly.

Kahoot! can be used with children as young as kindergarten because users select a colored shape on their device: red triangle, blue diamond, yellow circle, or green square. As long as a user can identify either a shape or color that corresponds to the answer, they can play along!

Kahoot! is a free, fun review (and assessment!) tool that can be used at the end of a family information night, for group lessons, and more! To get started, sign up with Kahoot! as a teacher. Creating an account is as simple as setting up an email and password or logging in via Google. To create your kahoot quiz, go to create.kahoot.it. Add your questions and answer bank. You can select one to four correct answers and set a timer for each question to ensure participants have enough time to respond. Kahoot! allows you to include a photo or even use a video clip as part of your question!

You can make questions worth points or not worth points. Sometimes the points are fun because you get to see a leaderboard. Users get points based on both accuracy and speed of responses. If the students are competitive or focused on the points and not the content, you may choose to not have the questions worth points. Points are a great tool to engage a group to participate who might not otherwise be excited by a review. For example, if you are hosting a financial aid information session for families, they might not stick around for a review, but you want them to participate so that you know what they retained. Telling families you are going to play a game (and maybe even offer prizes to the top three winners) is more likely to result in participation than if you share out a survey.

When explaining to participants how to get started, here are some helpful instructions:

1. Go to: kahoot.it
2. Type in Game PIN I give you.
3. Type in your FIRST NAME or an appropriate NICKNAME.
4. Join.

Be sure to freeze your projected screen (or don't project) until all participants join with appropriate names. You can kick out students with inappropriate names, but you wouldn't want that projected for all to see. To further engage an audience, you could also have them select the name of a favorite musician, cartoon character, athlete, and so on. Seeing these famous figures populate your kahoot leaderboard is a sure way to elicit laughter and engagement.

Kahoot! is often an entry point for school counselors using technology because they see the value of it when teachers use it, they can engage students and staff in a fun activity, and they are organically collecting data. It's free, easy to set up, and often students have used Kahoot! with teachers, which makes it easier for counselors since they don't have to explain how to go to the website, log in, and so on.

I'll take, "Checks every box for $1,000, Alex!"

NOTES

_____

_____

_____

_____

_____

_____

_____

_____

_____

_____

_____

_____

_____

GOOGLE FORMS

RECOMMENDED GRADE LEVEL	ELEMENTARY SCHOOL	MIDDLE SCHOOL	HIGH SCHOOL
LEVEL OF DIFFICULTY	EASY	MODERATE	A LITTLE MORE ADVANCED
COST	FREE	FREE TO USE PAY TO UPGRADE	FREE TRIAL PAY TO ACCESS

Google Forms could be used to create guided notes for instruction, create easy pre- and/or posttests, register students for events, collect and analyze school climate surveys, track counselors' use of time, and much more.

When most people talk about Googling it, the conversation starts and stops at the search engine. Google Forms is one of the first tools for any school counselor (and is one of the first tools any educator should learn to love). Using the same skills that we would use to make a simple questionnaire or survey, so much more can happen when using Google Forms.

The application can instantly collect, summarize, and analyze results. Forms can easily be distributed to other people by sharing the form directly, sharing the link, or using QR codes. Google Forms could be used to create guided notes for instruction, create easy pre- and/or posttests, register students for events, collect and analyze school climate surveys, track counselors' use of time, and much more.

Getting started is easy. The only thing you need is an email to register for a Google Account (see below). From there you're ready to go! From the Google Homescreen, you will access Google Drive. Google Drive can be accessed from "App Launcher" (the 9 dots in the upper right hand corner or the home screen) or by going to drive.google.com. Once at Google Drive screen, you'll see the NEW button in the upper left hand corner. Click on the button and select More, and you'll see Google Forms. You can also go to forms.new or docs.google.com/forms.

Getting Started With Google

To get started with Google, all you need is your name. (If you do not know your name, check your clothing for a form of identification or see if your name is written inside your garments, like on the underwear waistband.)

- Start by going to Google at www.google.com.
- In the upper right-hand corner you'll see Sign in.
- Click Sign in and then on Create account.
- Enter your name and username (acslater.baysidehs@gmail.com, albertslater 123@gmail.com, or your current email).

- Enter a phone number or email for recovery purposes (when you forget your password or to tighten up security).
- Enter your date of birth (so Google knows you're legally of age).
- Start Googling. The power of Gmail, Forms, Docs, Slides, Sheets, and much more is now at your fingertips. Google responsibly.

You're ready to go. You can make a Google Form from scratch (blank) or from a template:

1. Using a template will allow you to make easy contact forms, registration, or even T-shirt order forms.

2. Google Forms can be shared either by clicking the share document and sending the form, sharing the URL, or using a QR code.

3. Designing your own documents (like a registration forms) is as simple as writing a Word document. Questions can be formatted as open-ended short answers or paragraphs or different versions of preselected items (multiple choice, check-boxes, dropdown boxes, and various scaled responses). Respondents can even upload and submit files.

4. Questions can be grouped into sections and can be framed with written descriptions, pictures, and videos. Based off of individual responses, questions can be directed to different sections or groups of questions.

5. Responses can be analyzed simply by clicking on the response tab at the top of the form. See who submitted responses, see easy-to-read graphs based off of scaled responses, and so much more!

6. With practice, the use of Google Forms is only limited to the imagination and planning in the design and flow of information.

Google highlights several features developed by third parties. These services can be used in addition to the official Google Apps to create new elements. Using a Google Form add-on like Form Publisher, you could electronically record a senior survey and create a personalized document that could either be printed or shared electronically. Students could use the Google Forms to record their Holland Code following a career lesson and receive a personalized score report sent both to the students email and their guardians. The power of Google Forms in conjunction with the rest of the Google Suite of Apps cannot be overstated. Endless data, custom reports, automated communication, and easy workflow all start with using Google Forms.

A Recipe for a Use of Time Tracker Using Google Forms:

- 1 Google Form

- 30–40 Checkboxes breaking the day into 15-minute increments

(Continued)

(Continued)

- 1 Multiple Choice for Direct and Indirect Services and non-counseling tasks

- Another 2-3 Dropdown boxes listing some regular or recurrent tasks (lessons, groups, crisis response—direct) or (data analysis or program planning—indirect)

- 1 Short Answer for student's name, if applicable

- 1 Paragraph for Notes

Build the form with the fields above to create an easy Use of Time tracker. The Tracker will automatically break down and analyze your data.

NOTES

_____

_____

_____

_____

_____

_____

_____

_____

_____

_____

_____

_____

_____

_____

_____

_____

_____

_____

GOOGLE SHEETS

RECOMMENDED GRADE LEVEL	ELEMENTARY SCHOOL	MIDDLE SCHOOL	HIGH SCHOOL
LEVEL OF DIFFICULTY	EASY	MODERATE	A LITTLE MORE ADVANCED
COST	FREE	FREE TO USE PAY TO UPGRADE	FREE TRIAL PAY TO ACCESS

Sheets will automatically: read your data; analyze it; form charts, graphs, and pivot tables; and/or make summary statements about the data.

Let's fall in love with spreadsheets all over again. Educators revolt; let's reclaim the spreadsheet from the accountants! Google Sheets is the spreadsheet application from Google. Sheets can be a great resource for storing, organizing, categorizing, and analyzing data. Sheets can help users visualize data and patterns, crunch large number sets, and develop insights about a population.

How do you get started? The only thing you need is an email to register for a Google Account (see "Getting Started With Google," page 42). From the Google Homescreen, you will access Google Drive. Google Drive can be accessed from "App Launcher" (the 9 dots in the upper right-hand corner of the home screen), at drive.google.com. Once at the Google Drive screen, you'll see the NEW button in the upper left-hand corner. Click on the button and select "Google Sheets." You can also download and open the free app, or simply go to sheets.new or sheets.google.com.

Starting with Google Sheets is easy. A new spreadsheet can be started, or a type of spreadsheet can be selected from Templates. Users can select templates, including to-do lists, invoices, schedules, calendars, gradebooks, attendance rosters, and even assignment trackers. Data can be populated from a Google Form (see page 42), or imported from your computer from an .xlsx or .csv file.

Simple spreadsheet dragging can be used in Google Sheets, making data entry faster. Similarly, Sheets will count the number of items occurring across cells for you simply by highlighting the cells. By using the Filter button (the button that looks like a funny Y or a funnel), users can organize or pull specific sets of information or arrange the data into an alphabetical or numerical sequence. Spreadsheet formulas like =SUM, =AVERAGE, =MEDIAN, and more can quickly process and aggregate data sets. More advanced features like combining cells, such as a student's FIRST NAME in Column 1 and LAST NAME in Column 2, can happen with the formula =CONCATENATE.

The most important features of Google Sheets are the more subtle ones. One example is appreciated by anyone who has ever used a spreadsheet: The document automatically saves and archives. Any deletions of partial or complete datasets can be restored or retrieved through the archive by clicking on the

"All Changes Saved in Drive" button at the top of the screen in the middle. Collaboration with colleagues to edit, share, or view the spreadsheet is easy with the Share button; the whole sheet or individual rows, columns, or cells can be protected from editing.

Finally, while there isn't an Easy button, the Explore button in the lower right-hand corner provides ease in data analysis and exploration. Using the robust artificial intelligence resources of Google, Sheets will automatically read your data; analyze it; form charts, graphs, and pivot tables; and/or make summary statements about the data.

The use of Google Add-ons (page 52), combined with Google Forms, can create sophisticated systems of information gathering, automation, and analysis. Email can be triggered and generated from Google Sheets, and information from the spreadsheet can be used to make the email appear personalized. The options with Google Sheets can be truly endless with a little experimentation and without the need for any advanced training or education in computer science or statistics.

**Did You Know That You
Can Use Google Sheets to Print Posters?**

1. In a new Google Sheet, in the Insert menu, select "image" to add your .jpg or .png photo.

2. In the View menu, zoom out to 50%.

3. Select your image and drag it by the bottom right side to enlarge it to cover the rows and columns you see on your screen.

4. Select print, and when the print menu comes, select "custom page breaks." You might have to zoom out to see the breaks, which indicate how the pages will print out. Move the adjustable lines to where you feel the best page breaks should be so that the image prints out in a more cohesive manner. For example, you probably don't want a page break on someone's face.

5. Print your pages and use a paper cutter (or very steady hand) to trim the white parts of the paper to only show the printed image.

6. Use spray adhesive to glue the image together on a large piece of poster paper. Alternatively, you can flip the pages over so they are face down and tape them together in the back. Don't use stick glue or liquid glue because it makes the paper look bubbly and not smooth.

Hint: If you want a larger poster, zoom out more and drag the image across more cells to enlarge it.

Reminder: Be mindful of copyright issues and similar consideration when creating your poster.

PLICKERS

RECOMMENDED GRADE LEVEL	ELEMENTARY SCHOOL	MIDDLE SCHOOL	HIGH SCHOOL
LEVEL OF DIFFICULTY	EASY	MODERATE	A LITTLE MORE ADVANCED
COST	FREE	FREE TO USE PAY TO UPGRADE	FREE TRIAL PAY TO ACCESS

One of the more difficult tasks school counselors have is to quantify their impact. Plickers (plickers.com) is a simple way to gather mass quantifiable data without distracting students with technology. Plickers is a quizzing application that allows you to ask questions to a group and gather responses in seconds with the use of your cell phone camera.

Teachers use Plickers in the classroom for pop quizzes or to test the understanding of concepts throughout a lesson, and counselors can use Plickers in their school counseling lessons as a pre- and/or posttest or to measure the comprehension of concepts, perceptions, and beliefs about topics based on participant responses to questions.

> The American School Counselor Association (ASCA) *School Counselor Professional Standards & Competencies* (2019) "outline the mindsets and behaviors school counselors need to meet the rigorous demands of the school counseling profession and the needs of pre-K–12 students." An effective school counselor and comprehensive school counseling program uses data to support decision making for effective programming and interventions, improving services for students.

Plickers can also be used in a group counseling session to quickly collect data in a more engaging manner than handing out another survey. It ensures that all students are participating while allowing respondents to give their answers privately and without judgment or to track the growth of your audience. Rather than relying on the response of one or two people, Plickers allows you to get a snapshot of the entire group.

Plickers can also be used with staff and families to collect responses during and after sharing out information. School counselors are often in a position to provide staff professional development, particularly in areas such as mandating reporting of suspected child abuse. Counselors also provide information to students and families in sessions about course selection and financial aid and share strategies and resources to support the social-emotional growth of children at every developmental level. Plickers supports audience participation and guides counselors to know which topics to dive deeper into while seamlessly collecting data.

Gathering results when using Plicker requires the use of a smartphone or tablet because the app needs access to your camera:

1. Registering requires an email and password to give you free access.

2. On the menu bar, select Classes and enter your students. This allows the site to assign a Plickers card to each student.

3. Select the Cards tab on the menu bar to print out individual Plicker cards for your students.

    Note: Plicker Cards can be reused in other classrooms; regular printer paper may not last as long as the cards exchange hands. Using heavier paper and/or matte laminating is advised. Laminating allows you to wipe down cards between uses to prevent the spread of germs

4. Select the library tab to enter true-false or multiple-choice questions.

5. Display the question and real-time answers by selecting the Live View tab if you have your tablet, smartphone, or computer connected to a projector or smart screen.

6. Students should hold up their Plicker card to answer the question. Be sure the current question is up on your smartphone or tablet and use the camera to scan the classroom and gather students' responses.

Plickers utilizes printable cards to gather students' answers. The Plickers cards are unique QR codes the app reads to identify which student is responding to the question. For the app to know how the student is responding depends on how the student has the card oriented. As you may be able to see in the image, numbers and letters are on the perimeter of the code. The number coordinates with the assigned student number on the class roster, and the letters A, B, C, and D are possible responses to multiple-choice questions or A and B for true-false questions. Whichever letter is at the top of the student's card is their response to the question. The letters are tiny so students must come up with their own answer; they won't be able to look around the room at how the majority of the class is responding.

The real benefit of Plickers is beyond the use in classrooms and groups. The reports tab allows you to manipulate and analyze your data. Show trends, intervention results, and student-specific data. Reports can be filtered by class, question, student, and timeframe. You can print individual reports or export your data to Excel. Exporting allows you to further analyze your data with graphs or share results with others. You can also archive reports to access at a later time. This allows you to remove the data from an analysis without fully deleting it.

Finally, Plicker currently can only support up to 63 different students, meaning only 63 numbered cards. This can be an issue if you are doing a large audience presentation. To troubleshoot this, you can create multiple classes for one presentation and identify them by location (e.g., *front of room, left side, right side, back of room,* etc.). Simply assign the students to a number and location. You will have to change classes in the app before scanning each portion of the room.

SOCRATIVE

RECOMMENDED GRADE LEVEL	ELEMENTARY SCHOOL	MIDDLE SCHOOL	HIGH SCHOOL
LEVEL OF DIFFICULTY	EASY	MODERATE	A LITTLE MORE ADVANCED
COST	FREE	FREE TO USE PAY TO UPGRADE	FREE TRIAL PAY TO ACCESS

Socrative (socrative.com) is great for quick assessments, exit questions, longer quizzes, and fun review games! You can assign individual game-based reviews or have students work together in groups. Students don't need to have an account. They can enter your classroom with a code you give them.

The unpaid access gives you 50 students per session and one public room for your class, which is perfect for school counselors. It also gives you access to the Space Race assessment, which is a favorite feature for students!

School counselors are using Socrative for self-directed learning experiences based on career-related topics:

- **Career search:** The University of Missouri's Career Center offers a free online Career Interest Game (career.missouri.edu/career-interest-game). Counselors guide students toward this website to learn more about personality and career fit based on the Holland Code. The website links careers to O*NET (onetonline.org) for further career exploration and job analysis.

- **College:** Create a self-directed webquest for students to identify the cost of tuition at a local university, community college, or tech school.

- **Military:** Refer students to specific websites about the benefits of joining the military. Create a Socrative quiz with questions to guide students to respond to specific and the most important benefits of joining the military.

- **Digital Citizenship and Cybersecurity:** Guide students toward specific links on websites like commonsensemedia.org. Provide specific questions around digital citizenship or cybersecurity that can be addressed by exploring links.

Socrative is primarily used by teachers as a review tool, and school counselors are increasingly using it for classroom lessons and group work. Here are some steps to get started on a sample lesson:

1. Set up an account as a teacher. You'll need an email address and a password.

2. Create a multiple choice quiz by selecting "create quiz" and "multiple choice." You'll notice that you can customize the number of responses and also have a space to provide feedback to students.

3. Enter your questions, responses, and feedback to students.

4. Each question can be anchored to state-specific competencies and standards. Simply by selecting a state, each response can be tied to a common core or other state-level educational standards.

Sample question: Go to the Occupational Outlook Handbook on the Bureau of Labor Statistics (bls.gov/ooh). Under the Browse Occupations menu, select Most New Jobs (Projected).

Which occupation is listed in the top 5?

Options: software developer, accountant, air traffic controller, veterinarian

---

To share your quiz with students:

1. Select the Launch menu and then the Space Race icon.

2. Select your quiz; there are several options to choose from.

3. Divide students into teams and assign a lead who will be the person with the device. The colors for teams are predetermined, so four teams would be blue, magenta, lime, and peach.

4. Before you launch, determine the number of teams, look at the colors for that number, and preassign students to groups based on the Socrative color coding.

Under the icon menu, you can select from the spaceship or another item or animal. Once you launch, the fun begins! Counselors are using Socrative to encourage self-directed learning about a variety of topics. Guide students to preselected resources about careers, internet safety, conflict resolution, and so on. Your questions should be directly tied to these resources so students can find answers.

The students' icons move forward by team (color) for correct answers, and they don't move for incorrect answers. In other words, they don't move backward. They also get feedback on their responses. Students have reported that they enjoy these types of learning activities because the emphasis with Socrative is on accuracy and not speed. It also mimics their natural investigation strategies if they are looking for information online.

To review a spreadsheet of responses, select "reports," and then select your quiz to download files. If you find there is a pattern of difficulty or great ease, you can adjust your lesson accordingly. Counselors can use the data in responses as an advocacy tool and to drive funding of programs.

For example, if counselors use Socrative after assemblies on critical topics, they can quickly learn which messages or themes resonated with students. One counselor shared that she used Socrative to review important messages after an antibullying assembly. The speaker was engaging and entertaining, but the data from responses showed that students recalled the jokes and antics and didn't retain the important messages. The counselors used the data to support changing the annual speaker, and the following year they compared the data from the new speaker to the previous one to demonstrate the value of the change and continued funding.

Students are searching the web for information regularly. Socrative provides a platform for counselors to use these real-life skills to address school counseling–related topics in a collaborative manner.

NOTES

_____

_____

_____

_____

_____

_____

_____

_____

_____

_____

_____

_____

_____

_____

_____

_____

_____

_____

_____

_____

_____

_____

_____

_____

_____

_____

_____

_____

_____

GOOGLE ADD-ONS

RECOMMENDED GRADE LEVEL	ELEMENTARY SCHOOL	MIDDLE SCHOOL	HIGH SCHOOL
LEVEL OF DIFFICULTY	EASY	MODERATE	A LITTLE MORE ADVANCED
COST	FREE	FREE TO USE PAY TO UPGRADE	FREE TRIAL PAY TO ACCESS

> Using Google Add-ons has streamlined my accountability and management practices, giving me more time to work with individual students.
>
> —Dana Wile, school counselor, Penn Manor High School, Lancaster, PA

Google Add-ons is the term used to describe features of G Suite products developed by a third party. The add-ons can range from simple hacks to feats just short of magic. The add-ons work with Google Slides, Docs, Sheets, and Forms. They are mini-apps inside each of the Google apps. Officially called "editor add-ons," the mini-services are accessed at the top menu of Slides, Sheets, and Docs under "Add-ons" and under the puzzle piece at the top of the screen in Google Forms. New features or resources can be added, or the add-ons make G Suite apps work in new and interesting ways.

Under the Add-ons menu, the mini-apps can be activated, similar to turning on spell-check or inserting a pic. New add-ons can be found and added under the same menu, with the exception of Forms, which keeps add-ons under the hamburger menu. The add-ons can be removed or issues can be reported to the developer under "Manage add-ons." Nearly all the add-ons are free.

There are many existing and emerging add-ons for the G Suite products. A few examples include:

- Slides add-ons can enhance the quality of a presentation, adding more pictures, formative assessments, or building in a table of contents automatically.

- Docs has great add-ons features like including easy bibliography and citations[1], a writing coach, or even an embedded player to watch a YouTube tutorial while you're writing.

- Google Sheets add-ons can remove duplicates on a spreadsheet, automatically take the contents of a sheet to form an email, or produce convenient mail merges.

- Google Forms add-ons can create auto-generated confirmation emails, PDFs from response, or autocorrect the Google Form as a test or quiz.

---

[1]Me (2018). *Google Add-ons Are Awesome to Make Real or Example Citations: This Book.* Some City, CA: Textpub.

The true power of Google Add-ons is in the rich interaction between the G Suite apps. Student responses to a schoolwide survey via Google Forms can be instantly processed via Google Sheets and produce a personalized email back to the students using Google Add-ons. During a presentation or lesson using Google Slides, participants could provide live feedback via Google Forms. Information on students could be incorporated into a report written in Google Docs from a .csv file uploaded to Google Sheets.

Experimentation and creativity are the keys to transforming Add-ons into limitless potential. Google is transformed from basic search to cutting-edge technology, where the borders of productivity and automation can truly be pushed.

NOTES

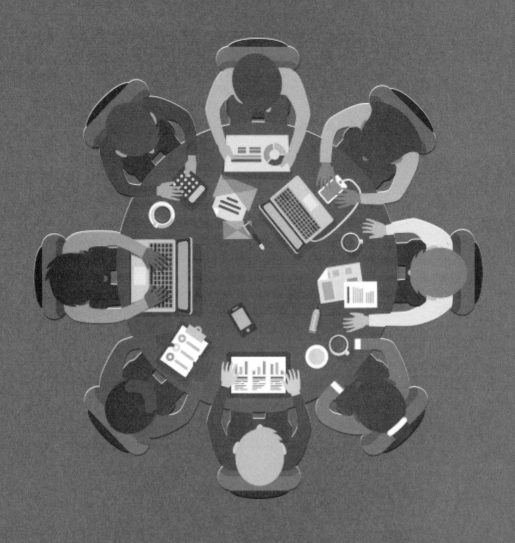

PART III

ORGANIZATIONAL TOOLS

GOOGLE KEEP

RECOMMENDED GRADE LEVEL	ELEMENTARY SCHOOL	MIDDLE SCHOOL	HIGH SCHOOL
LEVEL OF DIFFICULTY	EASY	MODERATE	A LITTLE MORE ADVANCED
COST	FREE	FREE TO USE PAY TO UPGRADE	FREE TRIAL PAY TO ACCESS

Are you a to-do list maker? Do you have little scraps of paper cluttering your desk with little reminders and notes? Do you want to find a better organizational system so you don't ever again have to worry about that lost sticky note? Then Google Keep is the organizational tool you are looking for!

Google Keep has some fantastic organizational features! You can create a series of notes, each with its own title. Your notes can have a list of items, addresses, links to websites or documents, photos, and so much more! You can color-code your notes and even add a photo heading. You can share a note with others (who can edit it) and set reminders for each of your notes.

School counseling departments have used Google Keep to create task lists for projects such as planning a career day. Counselors can work collaboratively to check off items as completed and see what else needs to be done.

Sharing the notes is beneficial when several people are working on a project. School counseling departments have used Google Keep to create task lists for projects such as planning a career day. Counselors can work collaboratively to check off items as completed and see what else needs to be done. When everyone has access to the same to-do lists, collaboration is super simple because the changes one person makes is reflected in the shared Google Keep notes.

Students use Google Keep to keep track of assignments. They create notes for each class and set an alert to go off at a time when they are in each class to remind them to write down homework. When they get home and complete assignments, they can mark items as completed, and if the note is shared with family member, that person can see that the student is keeping track of assignments. Students can also set an alert by location. A reminder can pop up when they are at home, at the library, and so on to help students remember that homework is the priority.

Many educators have found that Google Keep is beneficial on a personal level to reduce home stress. Sharing notes with family titled "Grocery List," "Chores," or the like ensures that family members can add to the list and cross items off as purchased or completed. For example, a parent reported that her teenage son kept saying he forgot to do his chores and simply didn't see paper notes of reminders when he got home. The teen insisted he was simply a forgetful person. The parent and teen started using Google Keep with reminders of what needed to be done when he got home. The pop-ups on his phone (which the parent can edit as needed) prompted the forgetful teen to take out the trash, defrost chicken for dinner, start his homework, and so on.

Get started today! Download the app for free on your phone (iOS or Android) or go to keep.google.com. Connect to your Google account. Get started by adding your first note. You need a title and then can add more notes.

NOTES

LIVEBINDERS

RECOMMENDED GRADE LEVEL	ELEMENTARY SCHOOL	MIDDLE SCHOOL	HIGH SCHOOL
LEVEL OF DIFFICULTY	EASY	MODERATE	A LITTLE MORE ADVANCED
COST	FREE	FREE TO USE PAY TO UPGRADE	FREE TRIAL PAY TO ACCESS

LiveBinders is an e-portfolio to house any web-based or digital materials, what the developer refers to as a "three-ring binder for the web." The site can be an excellent resource to store a range of digital material for later use. LiveBinders can be used to share, reflect, or collect educational tools.

LiveBinders is free to use, allowing users to keep up to five binders, with two levels of tabs. The premium plan allows users unlimited binders and up to three levels of tabs for a fee.

Going to www.livebinders.com allows users to sign up with only an email address or using their Google account. Once logged in, you're ready to begin. By clicking on New Binder, you're ready to start. Each binder has tabs at the top of the page; clicking on each tab will allow you to title the tab. The charm of LiveBinders is the ease of adding content. URLs for a website, resource, or streaming media can be added to the binder page, opening up on the binder page. Users can also upload their own media or files directly into a binder page by clicking on the + Content button at the top of the page; text can be written onto binder pages using the Content button, too. Additional tabs can be added horizontally like adding pages to a book. Subtabs, which can be added vertically, guide viewers deeper into the content of the subject of page.

LiveBinders, once completed, can be shared by clicking on the share tab. The binders can be shared via email address, social media, or even Google Classroom. Binders can also be assigned via email with permission granted to view or edit.

LiveBinders can be a go-to destination for almost all things counseling. The dust-covered binders can be dropped from the shelves, while LiveBinders can be used to store lesson plans, program resources, old newsletters, and other materials.

Occasionally, resources don't upload seamlessly or aren't viewable on a binder page; but the product still feels as easy to use as making a real-world scrapbook. Whether it is for a student portfolio, information binder for training, or parent education, LiveBinders are an easy way to maximize online resources.

YOUCANBOOK.ME

RECOMMENDED GRADE LEVEL	ELEMENTARY SCHOOL	MIDDLE SCHOOL	HIGH SCHOOL
LEVEL OF DIFFICULTY	EASY	MODERATE	A LITTLE MORE ADVANCED
COST	FREE	FREE TO USE PAY TO UPGRADE	FREE TRIAL PAY TO ACCESS

YouCanBook.me (youcanbook.me) is appointment booking software that integrates with your Google or iCloud Calendar. You set the dates, times, and appointment length and even padding between appointments. Users can select an available time to make an appointment with you. They automatically get notifications and reminders about the time they booked and can even reschedule for another time.

When someone books an appointment with you, you will receive an email with the details, and the appointment is automatically slotted in your Google or iCloud calendar. The automation of reminders to users and addition of the appointment to your calendar makes YouCanBook.me a real time-saver and helpful organizational tool.

Although you can sign up with an email address, we recommend you sign up with Google or create an account with iCloud. The integration with your existing online calendar is key.

Once you sign up, select the dates and times you want to be available for appointments. You aren't giving users access to your entire calendar; you set up the times you want to be available for appointments. You can also adjust these times if your schedule changes. For example, if you'd like families to sign up to meet with you, you can set aside Tuesday for afternoon appointment availability and Thursday for morning appointment availability. This makes it really easy for families to select a time and date that works for them without a lot of back-and-forth coordination. You can also change your availability when school events or holidays make those dates unavailable.

Jim and Cindy Walsh have just moved from Minnesota to California. They want to meet with the school counselor to learn more about the high school their twins Brenda and Brandon will attend. They can easily make an appointment with the counselor because the counselor's website has a link to YouCanBook.me! Jim and Cindy appreciate that they can select a date and time that works with their schedule.

Many educators get started with YouCanBook.me for specific events, such as Back-to-School night or family-teacher conferences. Back-to-School nights can result in lots of drop-in requests to meet, and using YouCanBook.me can streamline requests. During conference season, families may wish to make private appointments with educators to discuss sensitive matters. YouCanBook.me helps organize these requests. Educators enjoy the confidentiality of the program because users only see appointment availability and not who else has made an appointment.

Instructors at the university level have been using YouCanBook.me for years to organize office hours. Educators are increasingly seeing the value of booking software to organize their appointments with families and also with students. What a time-saver!

NOTES

_____

_____

_____

_____

_____

_____

_____

_____

_____

_____

_____

_____

_____

_____

_____

_____

_____

_____

_____

_____

_____

DOODLE

RECOMMENDED GRADE LEVEL	ELEMENTARY SCHOOL	MIDDLE SCHOOL	HIGH SCHOOL
LEVEL OF DIFFICULTY	EASY	MODERATE	A LITTLE MORE ADVANCED
COST	FREE	FREE TO USE PAY TO UPGRADE	FREE TRIAL PAY TO ACCESS

You want to plan a meeting. To pick a time everyone is available, you write an email listing several dates and times and send it out to colleagues. Then it begins. The responses (sometimes sent to only you and sometimes reply all) come flooding in. You are then tasked with reading all the email to find a date and time that works for everyone. On top of that, the responses are never simple and you are forced to read all the reasons why people can or can't make a certain time. Ugh. How did people even schedule meetings before email?

You want to plan a girls' night out with some friends you haven't seen in ages. To pick a time everyone is available, you write an email to your friends suggesting several dates and times that might work. Here we go again. There's got to be a better way to do this. Well, good news. There is!

Doodle (doodle.com) is a free website that simplifies scheduling a meeting at work, get-togethers with friends, or any other event in which several people have to find a date and time they are all available. We are all very busy, and Doodle makes the process of getting together with others a lot easier.

Signing up takes seconds. After filling out a form listing the name and location of your event, you need only list several dates and times (which is easy since you are just clicking on a calendar). This creates a link that is able to be shared with the meeting or event participants.

Email the link Doodle gives you to your colleagues; their names automatically populate the participants' section. It's easy for participants to fill out the form since all they do is put a check next to dates and times that work. Doodle color codes the chart with yes/no/ifneedbe and lists the number of responses of each at the bottom of the chart. It is that easy. You don't even need to sign up for an account!

For example, your California high school just registered a new student (Will) from West Philadelphia. Will's aunt and uncle (Philip and Vivian) want to ensure a smooth transition and would like to meet with their nephew's teachers. As the counselor arranging the meeting, you want to avoid a long email chain with the teachers asking about their availability. You send out a Doodle poll to determine several dates and times all the teachers are available over the next week. When you call Philip and Vivian to offer them several options for dates and times to meet, they are very impressed with your speedy response.

If mere thought of planning a meeting feels exhausting, give Doodle a try. It makes scheduling, and your life, a lot easier!

Get started by going to Doodle.com; enter the dates and times of your meeting. Be sure to only select times and dates that *you* are available! The next option is to select from a few more features. We like to select If Need Be because it allows respondents more flexibility. If you only offer yes/no, more people are likely to select no.

Once you email the link to people you are inviting to the meeting, they can respond. They do not need to sign up for an account to respond! This is a major selling point for Doodle. You can get alerts for when people are responding. You can review responses and select a time that works best for everyone.

NOTES

_____

_____

_____

_____

_____

_____

_____

_____

_____

_____

_____

_____

_____

_____

_____

_____

_____

GOOGLE CALENDAR

RECOMMENDED GRADE LEVEL	ELEMENTARY SCHOOL	MIDDLE SCHOOL	HIGH SCHOOL
LEVEL OF DIFFICULTY	EASY	MODERATE	A LITTLE MORE ADVANCED
COST	FREE	FREE TO USE PAY TO UPGRADE	FREE TRIAL PAY TO ACCESS

It's time to ditch the paper calendar.

Google Calendar is the electronic calendar service hosted by Google. The online calendar allows users to track dates, important occasions, and appointments. The calendar will provide notifications on calendar events, and there are a range of features for organization, communication, connectivity, and convenience. Ditch the paper calendar.

Users have access to Google Calendar simply by setting up a Google account. They can access Google Calendar through the App Launcher, by going to calendar.google.com, or by downloading the app for Android or iPhone.

Google Calendar is an online calendar; it can never be lost, stained, or damaged and it does not need to be purchased every year. The calendar has the ability for users to send or receive invitations electronically to events and receive email notifications of events. Calendar events can have notes or agenda attached, including a website or URL. Calendar events can be added by a simple click on a box on the calendar. Times can be adjusted by clicking and dragging on the event. Users can type a quick title to add an event or click More Options.

From More Options, additional users can be added by adding an email address under Guests. You can look up the best time by clicking on Find a Time in the middle of the calendar event, allowing you to see the availability of all the guests. Users can also make the meeting a Google Hangout (page 100) by clicking on Hangouts on the calendar invite. If the meeting is a recurring meeting like a staff meeting, users can select the frequency of occurrences in the drop-down menu. You can create calendar events for meetings you don't attend by clicking on change owner and sharing ownership with another guest. Users using G Suite services also have the option of blocking out appointment slots and receiving notifications via text message.

In addition to sharing the calendar event with others, Google Calendar allows users to create additional calendars. You can keep a personal calendar, work calendar, family calendar, and one for the soccer team you coach, each with its own color coding! On the left side of the screen is an option, Add calendar. Here users can search for a contact or friend by typing in their name, subscribe to a calendar via URL, import a calendar file (like iCal), or search for calendars of interest (like holidays or sports schedules).

A major advantage of the digital calendar is that it syncs across devices to provide counselors with reminders that can pop up on their computer, phone, or even watch. Counselors who get caught up in work, conversations, or other activities find the reminders extremely beneficial and use them not only to remind them of meetings but also to make copies of handouts for lessons, to put out passes for students, or to follow up with a teacher or student. Many counselors say the reminders for self-care are helpful to prompt them to eat lunch, go to the restroom, and take a moment to simply take a few deep breaths.

You can share specific calendars with other people via email by going to the calendar settings and selecting the option to share the calendar with others. You'll need to know the email address of anyone you would like to share your calendar with. From settings you can also make the calendar public and allow for the calendar to be added to a website through an embedded code or directly onto a Google site with just a click of the Calendar button. Users can also set up notifications for invitations, meeting changes, and responses to invitations and receive notifications every morning with an agenda for the day. Google Calendar is able to be synced with iCal for iPhones by adding Google to accounts and passwords on your iPhone or iPad. Google Calendar is a great online calendar, allowing users the flexibility of scheduling appointments and meetings both in person and virtually with ease.

The versatility to use Google Calendar across platforms allows Calendar to:

- Schedule by typing into Google Search things like "Schedule a Lunch Appointment for Thursday at noon"

- Ask Google Assistant to summarize your agenda or book a meeting

- Use services like Google Add-ons or IFTTT to create interactions with other web-based services to book and schedule or track occurrences on your calendar simply by using your email, Twitter, or text messaging

Such broad and seamless interactions automating or streamlining processes like setting up meetings, tools for notification, and integration across platforms push the fossilized paper calendar close to extinction.

NOTES

_____

_____

_____

_____

_____

_____

_____

_____

_____

_____

GENIUS SCAN

RECOMMENDED GRADE LEVEL	ELEMENTARY SCHOOL	MIDDLE SCHOOL	HIGH SCHOOL
LEVEL OF DIFFICULTY	EASY	MODERATE	A LITTLE MORE ADVANCED
COST	FREE	FREE TO USE PAY TO UPGRADE	FREE TRIAL PAY TO ACCESS

Your brilliant yet clumsy student Steve has yet again spilled juice on his computer, fried it out, and didn't submit his letter on time. He says, "Did I do that?" and you know that is his cry for help. You have to scan his letter of acceptance to his dream college, but there is a long line at the copier. The teachers are anxiously watching the clock in the hopes of getting their copies made before prep ends. You can wait it out until the bell rings, but the next round of teachers will rush the copier.

There is no need to wait in line if all you need to do is scan documents! Download the free app Genius Scan (thegrizzlylabs.com/genius-scan), available on Android and iOS, and you'll have a scanner in your pocket! There are several free scanner apps, but this is the most user-friendly one with the clearest images. You can scan one page or a batch of several pages and email them to yourself or someone else.

With so many scanning apps, why are school counselors turning to Genius Scan? The images are very clear, they can easily take photos of documents or "scan" documents from photos they've already taken, and there is a generous limit of documents to keep on their server. You can edit and label your documents with ease, and there are no annoying advertising pop-ups in the free version.

I love that I can easily scan any hard copy document to create a PDF that I can then share via email, text, et cetera. I often use Genius Scan with other free apps like Adobe Acrobat to digitally fill out and sign various forms and documents.

—Bradley Fisher, Chicago, IL

Get started by downloading the app. Most people will start by scanning a document rather than using an existing image. To scan, select the icon of the camera and take a photo. You can scan just one page or a batch of pages. Select done and email the PDF to yourself or the person who needs the PDF! There are additional options for sharing, but we find the email option is the most versatile.

NOTES

IFTTT (IF THIS THEN THAT)

RECOMMENDED GRADE LEVEL	ELEMENTARY SCHOOL	MIDDLE SCHOOL	HIGH SCHOOL
LEVEL OF DIFFICULTY	EASY	MODERATE	A LITTLE MORE ADVANCED
COST	FREE	FREE TO USE PAY TO UPGRADE	FREE TRIAL PAY TO ACCESS

If This Then That (IFTTT) is the automation system for your digital life. IFTTT uses applets and services to connect apps, social media accounts, email, websites, and web-enabled devices in novel and interesting ways. An applet is a small application or program that connects two or more devices or apps together (e.g., share your Facebook profile pic with your Twitter profile pic). Each applet runs by starting with a trigger (IF THIS—my Facebook profile pic is changed . . .), it will THEN perform an action (. . . change my Twitter profile pic to match THAT).

There are many web-based services people interact with daily from YouTube, Facebook, email, SMS (text messages), and much more. The use of applets to trigger actions on the many web-based services partnered with IFTTT are called *services*.

IFTTT can automate your Twitter account, connecting, retweeting, and responding to users without picking up their phone or keyboard. Hashtags can be automatically tracked and stored. The website provides collections of Applets to help find the right applets, like those to support Apple or Android users, themes like politics, or even specific professions like educators.

Some of our Favorite Applets:

- Automatically share your new (YouTube) videos to your Facebook page

- Allow YouTube likes to become tweets

- Automatically thank new (Twitter) followers

- Track your work hours in iOS calendar

- Get the weather for the next day before we go to sleep

Data on tweets, posts, emails, and contacts can be automatically saved to your Google Drive or Sheets. Tweets, texts, hashtags, and calendar events can be archived to a spreadsheet. Imagine tracking your time and activity simply by using your calendar, and then a spreadsheet could tabulate your use of time and analyze for trends.

Are you retweeting a user too much or don't want to send a custom text message of "Coffee Run" to your work colleagues every time you pull into Starbucks? You can manage your applets on the My Applets tab. Here you can turn the applets on or off or delete them.

Track all your applets like automated tweets or email, Facebook page posts, archived journal articles received from the American Psychological Association, or when your WeMo Coffee Maker has brewed a pot through the Activity tab.

Logging in is easy using a Facebook or Google ID or email. If you sign in with an email, set your password and you're ready to go. The site will ask new users to pick at least three preferred services. Individual applets may need additional login depending on the service; you may need to log into your social media or other accounts to initially connect them to IFTTT.

Users can create their own applets using the IFTTT Platform. Platform will ask for information on your company, including name, website, approximate size, along with your name and role. Creating applets using Platform is as simple as selecting a trigger through a dropdown box (IF a new event is added to my iOS Calendar) and THEN selecting desired action from a dropdown box (THEN send me a SMS message). Certain actions can be customized, depending on the service.

IFTTT does a magic trick. Just like a stage magician through complex engineering, design, and architecture, IFTTT makes extremely complex interactions look simple. The versatility cannot be overstated.

IFTTT exists in the space between curiosity, creativity, and experimentation. While using daily tools like Facebook, YouTube, or Google, questioning "What would happen if they…" becomes more realized by the ease of the IFTTT tools. Simple interactions can begin with just a login and click of a virtual button; but with patience and imagination, some of the systems can become partially if not fully automated.

NOTES

_____

_____

_____

_____

_____

_____

_____

_____

_____

_____

_____

_____

_____

_____

SMALLPDF

RECOMMENDED GRADE LEVEL	ELEMENTARY SCHOOL	MIDDLE SCHOOL	HIGH SCHOOL
LEVEL OF DIFFICULTY	EASY	MODERATE	A LITTLE MORE ADVANCED
COST	FREE	FREE TO USE PAY TO UPGRADE	FREE TRIAL PAY TO ACCESS

Smallpdf is a seamless file conversion website allowing users to convert and modify files to or from PDF files. The portable document file (PDF) is a standard for business and education. PDFs are often preferred because they have small file sizes, they're easy to create, compatible between different operating systems, and can be interactive by adding links, media, and searchability. Reports, presentation slides, invoices, and notes are often distributed via the file form; but anyone who has ever tried to add a note or update the form knows the process is difficult.

Smallpdf allows users to convert PDFs to Microsoft Word documents for editing, updating, or remixing; the service can convert PDF tables to and from Microsoft Excel spreadsheets. Presentation slides and images can be converted to a Microsoft PowerPoint presentation or .jpg image.

Smallpdf offers a range of additional document services:

- Large PDF files can be compressed to a small size for storage or sharing.

- PDF files can also be combined or split using the service.

- PDF documents can be edited directly, trimmed, or rotated.

- Security features can also be added to documents like protecting the document or adding a signature.

- Simply read a PDF.

The best feature is one that will go unnoticed and never be seen. The company's privacy policy stresses user privacy, deleting documents (both original and converted) from servers every hour, and never viewing or analyzing the contents of the documents.

No login is required to use the service. Users can upload and convert up to two documents per hour. Paid plans allow members to use the service with no document limits, signature storage, ad-free service, and offline compatibility.

The use of the site is simple. Select the service you want to use, press the icon, then drag the file into the area that states "drop file here." You can also choose upload and select from the appropriate folder on your computer, or you can upload from file services like Google Drive or Dropbox. You can also download a Chrome extension for your web browser. The Chrome extension will automatically open the appropriate Smallpdf app when clicked on from the Chrome Menu bar.

Smallpdf is very useful for modifying and editing documents we handle on a regular basis. It can cut minutes or hours from new document creation, through simple downloads and re-edits. Smallpdf makes technically difficult file conversion tasks simple and quick. This leaves more time to focus on the actual content of the document or the messages trying to be conveyed.

NOTES

_____

_____

_____

_____

_____

_____

_____

_____

_____

_____

_____

_____

_____

_____

_____

_____

_____

_____

_____

_____

_____

_____

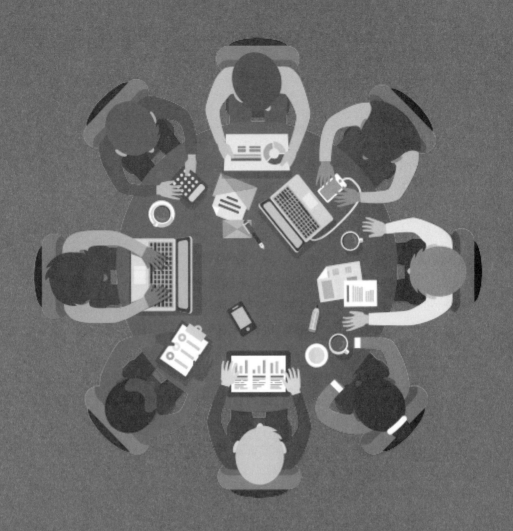

PART IV

PROGRAM PROMOTION TOOLS

REMIND

RECOMMENDED GRADE LEVEL	ELEMENTARY SCHOOL	MIDDLE SCHOOL	HIGH SCHOOL
LEVEL OF DIFFICULTY	EASY	MODERATE	A LITTLE MORE ADVANCED
COST	FREE	FREE TO USE PAY TO UPGRADE	FREE TRIAL PAY TO ACCESS

Remind is one of the simplest ways to engage families, keep them informed, and build connections.

Remind (remind.com) is a free text messaging app that educators use to communicate with students, families, and others in the school community quickly and easily. Recipients of messages don't need to have the app; they can receive information as a text message or email. Users can easily translate their message into another language to ensure they reach every family by selecting the globe icon. There are nearly 100 languages to choose from.

Remind messages are limited to 140 characters to support messaging across cell phone carriers. The shorter messages also increase the likelihood that recipients will read the message. Photos (of a flyer, for example) can be attached with more information or include a short link to a website to learn more.

Many educators have been using Remind for their classroom, clubs, and communicating during field trips. No longer is there is a need to pass around a spreadsheet with phone numbers of staff and chaperones. You can quickly send out announcements of where to meet up for buses (including a photo helps everyone spot the right location), morning reminders to pack a lunch, and share out about any last-minute changes.

School counselors use Remind by creating classes by grade level to target messaging. For example if you create a class for juniors (which includes both students and families), targeting juniors to attend a spring college and career fair, a photo of a flyer with more information can be included. Counselors can schedule messages to go out in advance and at a set time as an additional reminder before an event. Scheduling messages is a very helpful feature for announcements and reminders because you aren't tied to a device.

School counselors find that the greatest value is sharing information about local college open houses, scholarships, application deadlines, schedule changes, and even to send messages to individual students to get a quick reply without using their personal cell phone. Counselors can share office hours with families and students regarding their availability, which increases their accessibility and streamlines appointment scheduling. Remind is one of the simplest ways to engage families, keep them informed, and build connections.

The tech tool we are using a lot is Remind. We have created Remind classes for every grade level (high school 9–12). We have enabled the reply feature and that has been a life saver in answering questions, providing quick/brief information or links, and has increased our access to students/parents. It also allows us to meet students where they're at on the digital landscape.

—Eric Blanco, school counselor
from California

Get started by downloading the app or go to remind.com to sign up for an account. You create a class name and immediately begin adding members. Remind Support on YouTube has helpful tutorials, such as how to upload contacts into classes using a spreadsheet.

From the dashboard, you can start sending messages right away! You can also schedule messages and include links, handouts, photos, and other helpful information. With so many families and students having access to a cell phone, counselors have found that it's much more effective and efficient to reach people where they are—at their fingertips!

NOTES

_____

_____

_____

_____

_____

_____

_____

_____

_____

_____

_____

POWTOON

RECOMMENDED GRADE LEVEL	ELEMENTARY SCHOOL	MIDDLE SCHOOL	HIGH SCHOOL
LEVEL OF DIFFICULTY	EASY	MODERATE	A LITTLE MORE ADVANCED
COST	FREE	FREE TO USE PAY TO UPGRADE	FREE TRIAL PAY TO ACCESS

Create customized, fun, informative videos that stand out on any topic.

School counselors are often in a position to promote programs, advertise activities, and share out other important information. Standard ways of disseminating information with paper flyers and email sometimes means the message doesn't make it home or to the right audience. How can counselors cut through the information clutter?

Wow the crowd with animated videos you create using Powtoon (powtoon.com)! Create customized, fun, informative videos that stand out on any topic. Basic user accounts are free, but you can upgrade to get more optional features.

School counselors are using Powtoon to create videos to:

- Explain their role as a school counselor
- Provide students with information about emotional support services available to them
- Emphasize study skills, give educational tips, and provide other helpful information
- Inform students about clubs and other activities
- Provide information about upcoming events
- Request volunteer assistance and/or donations for school activities
- Explain to students and families the limits of confidentiality

ASCA Position Statement

"The School Counselor and Confidentiality"

The role of the school counselor regarding confidentiality is: . . . to inform students and the family of the limits to confidentiality when

- The student poses a danger to self or others
- There is a court-ordered disclosure
- Consulting with other professionals, such as colleagues, supervisors, treatment teams and other support personnel, in support of the student
- Privileged communication is not granted by state laws and local guidelines (e.g., school board policies)

- The student participates in group counseling

- Substance use and treatment are concerns (CFR, 42, Part 2; 2017) (ASCA, 1974, p. 23)

Creating a funny (yet informative) animated video allows counselors to share information in a way that the recipient is more likely to pay attention to and retain. The content is customized for the school, and counselors who might be shy about being on camera can still make a video with a cartoon figure of himself or herself without having to actually appear in it. Plus, if you want to make minor changes or update from year to year, you don't have to reshoot a video. Edits are simple!

This tech tool is so versatile that once you check it out, you will be very impressed with all it has to offer. If you have any difficulty, Powtoon offers great web-chat customer service and they are fantastic about responding to email from users in a timely manner and in a super-informative way. Some companies send auto-responses with suggested links to help you, but Powtoon has real people who are experts in the field responding to users.

To get started, sign up for a free account. You can sign up with Google, Facebook, or LinkedIn, or you can enter your email address and create a password. One of the first things you'll notice is that this is more of a business and marketing tool than a traditional education technology tool. School counselors are often in a unique role of marketing events, so tapping into a platform for this purpose is beneficial.

Watch a few videos to get a sense of the animation and play around! You might be surprised at how creative you can be and how fun the videos are to make. Once you finish your video, you are ready to share! You can share the video link or share it on social media.

NOTES

_____

_____

_____

_____

_____

_____

_____

_____

_____

_____

_____

_____

_____

CANVA

RECOMMENDED GRADE LEVEL	ELEMENTARY SCHOOL	MIDDLE SCHOOL	HIGH SCHOOL
LEVEL OF DIFFICULTY	EASY	MODERATE	A LITTLE MORE ADVANCED
COST	FREE	FREE TO USE PAY TO UPGRADE	FREE TRIAL PAY TO ACCESS

School counselors are often in a position to create flyers for events, photo collages from programs, and develop other promotional tools. Yet graphic design may not be in their toolbox of skills. What's a counselor to do?

Check out Canva (canva.com)! Its drag-and-drop platform allows you to design presentations and create eye-catching graphics, professional posters, stunning invitations, and more. Their free backgrounds, graphics, and layouts make it easy to get started. You can customize the fonts, add photo filters, and import free photos and clipart to spice up your design!

Canva saves you time, energy, and frustration with its easily customizable templates for a variety of platforms. Your school counseling department header for Twitter, your website, Facebook, and more are all different dimensions. Customizing one that fits perfectly and captures content is important, but it's terribly time-consuming to search the dimensions for each platform. Canva makes it easy to design for each platform.

In addition, you don't have to work in isolation as you create. Canva allows the user to make a free team for up to 400 members. One team member might upload logos and photos to use, another can add event details, and another can work on design. No longer will creation of promotional graphics rest on the shoulders of one staff member.

Canva is one of my most utilized online tools for posters, pamphlets, cards, and even parent and student letters. I find it simpler to navigate than some of the more popular software out there with hundreds of templates that make it easy to add my own touch to each document. My peers have asked me how I make the perfect posters and pamphlets for each event or project and I love telling them that it only took a few minutes on Canva.

—Kelsey Kman, school counseling MEd candidate, Pennsylvania

Get started by signing up on canva.com with just your email address and a password you create. You can immediately begin browsing nearly 50 templates. School counselors most commonly utilize templates for announcements, brochures, certificates, flyers, newsletters, photo collages, posters, and social media graphics. You'll find that many things you've been designing by hand are simplified and look so much more polished with Canva.

Canva is a very useful tool to customize printable organizing tools. You can create a planner for your day, week, or year. Simply customize by your school's time schedule and print! You can also create business cards and postcards. Many counselors use the postcards to send low-cost, customizable cards to students and teachers who are home sick for extended periods of time or going through a tough time.

Does your school's class schedule feel confusing for some students or require more time for new students to learn? Create a class schedule using Canva. This tool also helps students organize their schedules to incorporate before- and after-school activities. Counselors have printed out these schedules to use in organizational groups.

Canva is helpful as a digital and print resource for school counselors!

NOTES

PIC•COLLAGE

RECOMMENDED GRADE LEVEL	ELEMENTARY SCHOOL	MIDDLE SCHOOL	HIGH SCHOOL
LEVEL OF DIFFICULTY	EASY	MODERATE	A LITTLE MORE ADVANCED
COST	FREE	FREE TO USE PAY TO UPGRADE	FREE TRIAL PAY TO ACCESS

In the age of swiping and scrolling, images speak louder than words. Pic•Collage condenses several pictures into one ideal sized image for all social media outlets, allowing the viewer to see more in a single glance. Much like scrapbooking but on your smartphone or tablet, you can resize, move, and skew your pictures, adding words, stickers, and themed backgrounds to make your image stand out.

As a counselor, you want to engage your students in careers, positive mental health, and the resources you have to offer. Pic•Collage can be used as school counselor advertisements for upcoming programs and events, announcements, or fun reminders for upcoming deadlines. Share on any social media outlet without the fear of your image being distorted.

Do you want to take your photos to the next level? Use the animation feature to watch your photos move in a variety of patterns in the college. This is an exciting feature to use when you want to be sure you are drawing attention to your photo. It's especially useful for announcements and invites to events to grab the viewers' attention as they scroll through their social media feeds or scan your website.

Get started by downloading Pic•Collage for free on the Apple Store, Google Play, Windows Apps, and Amazon Apps:

1. Immediately enjoy creating, without setting up an account. Get started by making a card, using a premade grid or freestyle mode.

2. Select your photos, choose from a variety of backgrounds, and begin dragging, dropping, and resizing your photos. Add text and stickers to complete your project.

3. Save your image in My Collages, save it to your camera roll, or share it to your social media account.

As a counselor working in these tech-y times, Pic•Collage is the perfect way to grab the students' attention! I love that Pic•Collage is easy with their free platform, editing tools and the ability to share.

—Lisa Bruce, school counselor at College of Southern Nevada High School East

If you aren't sure how to start a project, select Explore in the app and scroll through others' creations. You can like and comment on designs and even follow accounts you get the most inspiration from. Follow @piccollage on Instagram or Twitter for inspiration on layouts.

Pic•Collage has hundreds of features to help make your collage original. While many of these features are free, Pic•Collage does have some features that are paid for. More intricate themes, backgrounds, and stickers can be directly purchased in the app. You can also register for the paid version of Pic•Collage, which removes the watermark from your images and opens up more features for your use.

NOTES

_____
_____
_____
_____
_____
_____
_____
_____
_____
_____
_____
_____
_____
_____
_____

BUFFER

RECOMMENDED GRADE LEVEL	ELEMENTARY SCHOOL	MIDDLE SCHOOL	HIGH SCHOOL
LEVEL OF DIFFICULTY	EASY	MODERATE	A LITTLE MORE ADVANCED
COST	FREE	FREE TO USE PAY TO UPGRADE	FREE TRIAL PAY TO ACCESS

Buffer is a social media management service. Buffer helps manage all things social media that arose after MySpace. Imagine you're a young emerging pop star with a trendy electronic synth band; you could post updates on gigs, new releases, and battles of the bands across Facebook, Twitter, and Instagram in minutes. Buffer is truly outrageous . . . truly outrageous! School counselors can use the tool for outreach to colleagues and sharing information to students or families. Buffer helps reduce the Babel effect, sharing across so many different mediums; it's almost like speaking a different language. With this one tool, time is freed while messages are quickly and consistently posted to the social media of the user's choosing.

Getting started is easy; all you need is an email address and to create your own password or to download the app on the Apple or Google Play store. Once you've logged in, Buffer will prompt you to connect your social media accounts. You will need to log in to the individual accounts through Buffer's connect buttons. Buffer allows for posts to social media like Twitter, Facebook Pages and Groups, LinkedIn, Instagram, and Pinterest (with a seven-day trial). The free version allows you to manage and post to three accounts, while the pro version allows up to eight (including Pinterest) for a fee.

From the Dashboard, click the blue Buffer button (it looks like a + sign). From there you can type in the content you wish to share, and add any pictures. Start by writing a post from your preferred social media account, for example Twitter. Write a post of up to 280 characters and consider adding a pic or two to grab your followers' attention. Links added will automatically be shortened using the default buff.ly URL shortener for the service, for instance www.jemandtheholograms.org would become buff.ly/2jrwtz. Don't worry, your link is still there; it just automatically changed to save you character length.

Once the post is completed, you can click on the icons for other social media accounts to automatically copy the post to the accounts—text, pictures, and all. Some platform-rich content, like hashtags, embedded links, or tagging, may be lost when sharing across multiple social media platforms at once. Still, Buffer can add content to Facebook Pages, Twitter, and LinkedIn simultaneously with only a few keystrokes. Buffer will even create an Instagram post that can be released later with a touch of the button.

A steady supply of tweets, posts, and updates can be scheduled days ahead of time and live online at the exact time of your choosing. Buffer can work with services like IFTTT (page 66) to automatically share your newest blog post across social media platforms, or even your latest YouTube video. Pop starlets can add content faster than rival bands like the Misfits or Stingers and barely touch any device (including their holographic computers). Counselors can schedule posts for events like parents' nights and FAFSA nights, weeks in advance; or automatically share school district information or resources through Buffer and the related services.

Buffer is a great social media management system for educators looking to increase their presence on social media or free up some time from posting content. The easy interface and application across platforms can really increase the scope of outreach and provide some uniformity at the same time.

NOTES

_____

_____

_____

_____

_____

_____

_____

_____

_____

_____

_____

_____

_____

_____

_____

_____

_____

_____

_____

_____

_____

_____

GOOGLE SITES

RECOMMENDED GRADE LEVEL	ELEMENTARY SCHOOL	MIDDLE SCHOOL	HIGH SCHOOL
LEVEL OF DIFFICULTY	EASY	MODERATE	A LITTLE MORE ADVANCED
COST	FREE	FREE TO USE PAY TO UPGRADE	FREE TRIAL PAY TO ACCESS

Google Sites needs no coding experience. The platform uses drag-and-drop features combined with the user's familiarity with other G Suite products to make professional quality websites.

Google Sites is the website building service powered by Google. With sleek design and the integration with Google services, Google Sites is a powerful tool in website development.

The only thing needed to get started is a Google account (see "Getting Started With Google," page 42). Then it's as simple as going to sites.google.com.

Google Sites needs no coding experience. The platform uses drag-and-drop features combined with the user's familiarity with other G Suite products to make professional quality websites. Sites can be built by clicking on the plus sign in the lower right-hand corner. Once a new site is open, it's ready to be edited. Clicking on the text box allows users to write; hovering over the lower part of Change Image can change the background image of the banner to one uploaded from your computer or downloaded from Select Image. Images can be uploaded from Google Drive or your Google albums, added via URL, or downloaded from the gallery or from the Search feature. Different styles of layout can be dragged right onto the web page. Text, images, and materials from Google Drive can be added directly to the page via the Insert tab. Additional resources like embedding a Google Form, YouTube video, a Slides presentation, Google Doc, published Calendar, or chart from Sheets is as simple as a click of a button and selecting the appropriate resource.

The combination of Google resources is both endless and seamless. College admission professionals can register via Google Form for a planned college fair or visit, or the events could appear on the Google Site via an embedded calendar. Student checklists or parent or guardian information sheets can be added directly to the site for easy communication and be accessible for a screen reader for students with visual impairments.

Similar to other Google products, Google Sites can be shared to build sites collaboratively or can be viewed with restrictions set by the site's owner. You can continue to check the quality of the site by clicking the Preview button, the button that looks like an eyeball at the top of the screen. The websites displayed from a phone, tablet, and desktop can be viewed by clicking between the three icons. Finally, when ready, the Site can be published with just a click of the Publish button. Users can change the URL to their liking. Free sites will be published as https://sites.google.com/view/ YOUR_URL_TITLE_WILL_GO_HERE. Privacy settings for the site can be set prior to publishing. After publishing, Google provides a guide to registering a custom URL under Settings.

Google Sites is an easy and free way to build clean and professional-looking websites. If users are already using some of the G Suite applications in their professional life, Google Sites is an obvious choice.

NOTES

_____

_____

_____

_____

_____

_____

_____

_____

_____

_____

_____

_____

_____

_____

_____

_____

_____

_____

_____

_____

_____

_____

_____

_____

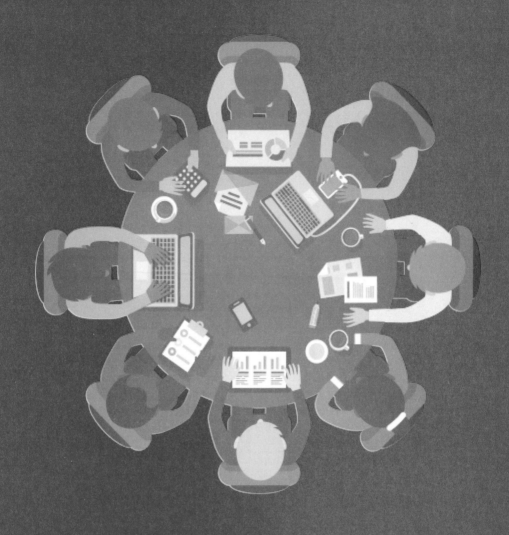

PART V

COLLABORATION
TOOLS

TWITTER

RECOMMENDED GRADE LEVEL	ELEMENTARY SCHOOL	MIDDLE SCHOOL	HIGH SCHOOL
LEVEL OF DIFFICULTY	EASY	MODERATE	A LITTLE MORE ADVANCED
COST	FREE	FREE TO USE PAY TO UPGRADE	FREE TRIAL PAY TO ACCESS

Twitter is one of the most underutilized free resources for educators. It helps you stay informed of current trends, share helpful resources, and connect with and collaborate with school counselors across the nation.

Twitter is your advocacy best friend! School counselors support students and staff, and they are experts in highlighting the accomplishments of others. You can use Twitter to support colleagues and promote your program! Many counselors find that taking photos of bulletin boards, events, and activities and sharing them via Twitter give administrators and the public insights into what they do. Often, the perception of school counselor roles is shaped from pop culture, and Twitter allows counselors to have a platform to promote the profession and innovative programs in their schools.

Twitter offers real-time information that helps counselors collaborate with other school counselors to proactively address issues. For example, a movie was released that sparked questions about suicide, sexual assault, and other intense topics. Families turned to school counselors for support, wondering about the right age for children to view the program and how to handle questions (questions that arose from children hearing about it and viewing it). Teachers turned to school counselors with questions about how to manage classroom conversations that centered around topics in the program. Administrators sought school counselors' advice on resources to put on district websites. Twitter provided a platform for school counselors to share questions they were receiving, how they were fielding them, and to seek support. Rather than feeling like we were reacting, we felt prepared to handle questions and be proactive with providing resources.

Getting started on Twitter is free and easy:

1. Set up a profile. Think of Twitter like your LinkedIn in that it's a public, professional presence that's discoverable by anyone. You'll want to use a professional-looking photo, and we recommend selecting a name (your Twitter "handle") that reflects who you are. For example, if you are a school counselor named Zach Morris, you can use names "CounselorZackMorris," or "ZackMorris123." There are many people on Twitter, so be prepared to select a creative name or to add numbers to your name to open your account.

2. Complete "About You." This is where you can list your professional affiliations, university, and any other things that describe you and your interests. For inspiration, check out some profiles of others in your role.

3. Follow people! Start with your national and state organizations. Take a look at who they are following to find key people to follow.

4. Use and follow hashtags. You'll find the key hashtags by looking at the tweets from your national and state organizations and also the people they follow. You can also search your job title on Twitter (e.g., "School Counselor," "School Social Worker," etc.). Check out this list for hashtags related to every area of interest.

5. You can also create "Lists" to manage groups of people you follow into specific themed feeds or conversations.

TweetDeck is a free, web-based platform that allows Twitter users to create columns to easily see the latest tweets from their favorite users or hashtags. The customizable columns eliminate the need to search for users or hashtags because it automatically refreshes. You can also use the columns to have direct access to your "Twitter Lists." Imagine waking up in the morning, sitting down to breakfast, and someone has opened your favorite newspapers and magazines to the pages where you can see the latest information on all the topics you care about. TweetDeck is the digital version of that.

Twitter Chats provide participants with an opportunity to engage with school counselors across the country about current trends in school counseling. You can share your ideas, learn great strategies, and hear about fantastic resources. School counselors know we can't do our job effectively, efficiently, or even ethically if we are working in isolation. Twitter Chats give us the opportunity to connect, collaborate, and meet other dedicated professionals for free!

Twitter users meet at a predetermined time to discuss a topic. Chats usually last 30 to 60 minutes and follow a structured Q&A format. Chats open with introductions (your name and role or job, where you are from). The moderator tweets "Q1" with a question and participants respond "A1" with an answer. ALL TWEETS include the Twitter Chat hashtag (#) at the end of each 280 character tweet.

> **Moderator:** "Q1 What is your favorite thing about being a school counselor? #SCCHAT"
>
> **Participant:** "A1 I love talking to students about career opportunities! #SCCHAT" To participate in the chat, you follow the hashtag (#) on Twitter. You can do this by searching #SCCHAT on Twitter. You'll want to keep refreshing your screen to see the latest tweets (be sure to select Latest in the menu).

I joined Twitter in 2014 and have found it to be an invaluable tool in helping me grow as a school counselor. Twitter allows me to be connected to and learn from thousands of educators throughout the country and around the world. By participating in school counselor chats (#scchat, #escchat, #mscchat), I have been able to network with other school counselors, teachers, administrators, and educational organizations by sharing my own ideas, accessing resources, and learning about new strategies, ideas, and topics that help me grow my comprehensive school counseling program and support students socially and emotionally, academically, and with postsecondary opportunities.

—Laura Ross, a current middle school counselor, former elementary school counselor, in Lawrenceville, Georgia, who focuses on connecting with students to connect them to their education

NOTES

_____

_____

_____

_____

_____

_____

_____

_____

_____

_____

_____

_____

_____

PADLET

RECOMMENDED GRADE LEVEL	ELEMENTARY SCHOOL	MIDDLE SCHOOL	HIGH SCHOOL
LEVEL OF DIFFICULTY	EASY	MODERATE	A LITTLE MORE ADVANCED
COST	FREE	FREE TO USE PAY TO UPGRADE	FREE TRIAL PAY TO ACCESS

The collective nature of Padlet allows people to initiate conversation on topics, and it helps the counselor identify themes.

Padlet is one of the most intuitive tech tools! Users feel like they are sticking notes on a corkboard using technology. Padlet demonstrates the value of using technology to enhance a paper practice.

School counselors have used Padlet in a variety of ways:

● **Feedback/Engagement**—Educators most frequently use Padlet to get information from students as part of a lesson. For example, are you creating a lesson for students and/or families about digital citizenship? Create a padlet and share the link to students and/or families to share concerns and questions. The collective nature of Padlet allows people to initiate conversation on topics, and it helps the counselor identify themes.

● **Introductions/Needs Assessment**—Create a padlet board and share the link with students. Ask them to upload a photo or video of themselves and share a little information about who they are and questions they may have about a topic (e.g., course selection). You can also use it as a staff introduction tool. Colleagues can share brief, fun tidbits along with a photo.

● **Digital Cards**—Do you have a student or colleague going through a tough time? Rather than passing around a paper card, users can contribute well-wishes via Padlet at their leisure. You can print out the page or share the link with the recipient.

● **Speaker Q&A**—Whenever you have a speaker come in, there is typically a Q&A time when the audience can ask questions. Have you had the experience of the Q&A time sounding like . . . crickets? Sometimes the audience is reluctant to speak up. Was a lot of information given and the audience needs time to process and formulate a question? Or maybe the speaker didn't cover every topic you anticipated. We love to use Padlet to collect audience questions while the speaker is presenting. We then curate and ask questions on behalf of the audience. This saves time and helps if there aren't a lot of questions since we fill in the time with our own questions.

● **Brainstorming**—Are you planning a big project at school like a talent show? You can organize the event and ensure that there is a good balance of performances. For example, if student Lisa Houseman can't decide between singing "I Feel Pretty" or "What Do the Simple Folk Do?," organizers can color-code proposals, add evaluators' comments, and make suggestions about which song might be a better fit. Many educators use Padlet to share thoughts and resources. Padlet allows you to post images, documents, videos, music, and files, and others can comment under the post.

Basic membership includes a few padlets and limits users by data usage. For most educators, this is a great way to test out the platform.

NOTES

_____

_____

_____

_____

_____

_____

_____

_____

_____

_____

_____

_____

_____

_____

_____

_____

_____

_____

_____

_____

_____

_____

_____

_____

FACEBOOK

RECOMMENDED GRADE LEVEL	ELEMENTARY SCHOOL	MIDDLE SCHOOL	HIGH SCHOOL
LEVEL OF DIFFICULTY	EASY	MODERATE	A LITTLE MORE ADVANCED
COST	FREE	FREE TO USE PAY TO UPGRADE	FREE TRIAL PAY TO ACCESS

Facebook (facebook.com) is a social networking website that has quickly become where many users go to for connecting with friends and family, getting recommendations, and staying in the know for just about everything. Out of the 328.3 million people in the United States (United States Census Bureau, n.d.), 214 million are on Facebook (Statista, 2018). This means that a majority of your students and their family members are on Facebook. It's important to keep a professional, appropriate presence on this platform and assume that a friend of yours may be connected to students or their family.

Your Facebook account can connect you to great professional resources and real-time feedback. ASCA's Facebook page shares current research that you can share and download, shows pictures and videos from recent conferences, and features work from school counselors across the country. Follow ASCA at facebook.com/AmericanSchoolCounselorAssociation

Use Facebook to connect with other school counselors. Share school counseling plans, creative resources, and see what counselors from different cities and states are implementing at their schools. Follow your favorite blogs' Facebook pages to get notified when they have new posts and *Like* pages that relate to education and online safety, so updates, posts, and articles show on your personal Facebook feed.

Follow the Savvy School Counselor for worksheets along with individual and group counseling activities (facebook.com/SavvySchoolCounselor). Follow and share the posts from The Helpful Counselor (facebook.com/TheHelpfulCounselor) and School Counselor World (facebook.com/pg/schoolcounselorworld) to engage your students and families in inspirational videos and current topics in the counseling field.

Get started collaborating and connecting on Facebook:

1. You can add a profile picture and cover photo, something that matches the theme of your personality. Remember that your profile photo and header picture are public by default and there is no way to change that.

2. Explore the privacy features on Facebook to select options that match your comfort level. For example, some counselors want to use Facebook for professional

purposes only and want posts to be public. Others use it for personal and professional networking, so they select to keep their profiles private. Remember that even with the strictest privacy settings selected nothing you post is ever 100 percent private. You may have mutual friends who can see things you share or comment on, and anyone can take screenshots.

3. Follow the American School Counselor Association (ASCA) and your state counselor organization for helpful and timely resources. For example, if there is a natural disaster in your area, ASCA and your state organization are likely to share articles and resources to help families. Linking these resources on your school website or sharing to staff and your school community via email can be very beneficial during a difficult time.

4. Follow your school's Facebook page to get connected with events and notifications in the school community.

5. When you log in to your Facebook page, you will first see posts, pictures, and videos your friends have shared, as well as a menu along the left side of the screen.

The Facebook groups can provide great support and resources. You'll find upticks in activities around certain times of the year (back to school) or if a national event impacts students. For example, if there is a death of a celebrity popular with teens, a national tragedy, or a new movie or TV series about mental health or counseling issues, you'll find lots of points of discussion and sharing of resources.

Before you post a question to the group, you can do a quick search to see if the topic was already thoroughly addressed by using the "search this group" search bar. You may find a wealth of resources!

Most people posting in the groups are looking for resources, organizational tools, lesson plans, and other ideas. Some may post for advice about specific situations, and this is where you need to refer back to the ASCA Code of Ethics (1974) and review confidentiality. People in the group can see who you are, and it's best to go into a post with the assumption that others will know who you are, where you work, and that someone close to your situation may see what you write.

Don't post, "I have a 12-year-old boy who has major hygiene issues. He comes to school in the same red sweatshirt and his curly hair is matted with grease. What should I do?"

Instead post, "Does anyone have resources for addressing hygiene concerns and possible underlying causes?"

The ASCA Position Statement "The School Counselor and Confidentiality" states, "*The role of the school counselor regarding confidentiality is: To support the students' right to privacy and protect confidential information received from students, the family, guardians and staff members.*"

WISESTAMP

RECOMMENDED GRADE LEVEL	ELEMENTARY SCHOOL	MIDDLE SCHOOL	HIGH SCHOOL
LEVEL OF DIFFICULTY	EASY	MODERATE	A LITTLE MORE ADVANCED
COST	FREE	FREE TO USE PAY TO UPGRADE	FREE TRIAL PAY TO ACCESS

Dear Dedicated Reader,

If you have made it this far in the book, you likely are eager to learn more about tech tools or you enjoy '90's movies references, corny humor, or both!

Email communication is the most common way educators interact with students and their families. Having a positive, informative email presence is critical when connecting with families and students. One of the best ways to demonstrate that you are a tech-savvy educator is to have an informative and concise email signature.

Without WiseStamp (wisestamp.com), many counselors have a lengthy, overwhelming signature because they want to include links to the counseling department's Instagram and Twitter handles, Facebook page, website, and more. Often, the signature is longer than the actual email message! Don't struggle with deciding what helpful resource to omit to shorten your email signature. WiseStamp signatures are concise and informative. They wow the viewer with linked icons and a concise, crisp, personalized layout that includes all your favorite resources that students and their families need.

> If you use a web-based email system (Gmail, Yahoo, AOL ← really?, or Hotmail), there is an awesome tool to help make your email signatures useful. Since most schools use Gmail if they use a web-mail service (sorry Outlook), we will focus on that. The tool we are talking about is called WiseStamp. It is a web plugin that allows you to customize dynamic and eye-catching email signatures. You can go basic or go nuts with what you want to put into your signature. If you are a super geek, you can even HTML code your own custom signature.
>
> —Jeff Ream, high school counselor and writer of *The Counseling Geek* at www.thecounselinggeek.com

WiseStamp is an email signature generator and Chrome extension (connects to your email). Users can sign up with one of three methods: standard email, Facebook, or Google login. The next step is to input your information and watch your signature come to life on the screen. There is no need to save and refresh to see what it looks like. Creating your email signature with WiseStamp takes about 5 to 10 minutes. Most counselors will create links to connect to their school's social media accounts and website rather than connecting to any personal accounts. Check with your school's policies, and follow their recommendations.

While the pay-per-month service gives you access to more options, it's completely possible to create an impressive signature using WiseStamp's free service. The branding on the bottom of your signature is discrete, and it can actually be beneficial to have it there since others will ask you about your new flashy signature and how they can get one. With the branding, they can simply click the link and get started creating their own WiseStamp signature.

Yours truly,
Angela Cleveland and Steve Sharp
Authors
Professional Nerds
Amateur Scrabble Players

NOTES

_____

_____

_____

_____

_____

_____

_____

_____

_____

_____

_____

_____

_____

_____

_____

_____

_____

_____

_____

_____

INSTAGRAM

RECOMMENDED GRADE LEVEL	ELEMENTARY SCHOOL	MIDDLE SCHOOL	HIGH SCHOOL
LEVEL OF DIFFICULTY	EASY	MODERATE	A LITTLE MORE ADVANCED
COST	FREE	FREE TO USE PAY TO UPGRADE	FREE TRIAL PAY TO ACCESS

Clarendon or Gingham? If these words resonate with you, you are likely an active Instagram user. Filters like these make Instagram a fun, engaging, photo-sharing platform and provide a major opportunity for program promotion without requiring expert photography skills.

School counselors are using Instagram to promote their programs and share uplifting pictures to the school community. Many school districts now have social media accounts and hashtags. School counselors often elevate the positive things happening in the schools by sharing out photos of great bulletin boards, exciting school events, examples of community-building activities, and more! The families may primarily see what's happening in their child's classroom or on their team if they follow a specific teacher or team. School counselors who have the ability to share out about all the wonderful things happening in the school and community on Instagram provide an engaging glimpse into the school as a whole.

Looking for inspiration from your counseling colleagues? You can follow key hashtags and engaging counselors on Instagram! You'll notice themes at certain times of the year. Before school starts, expect to find counselors posting pictures of their school counseling spaces and organizational ideas for the new year. The first week of February results in lots of posts about "National School Counseling Week" because

Instagram is the best way to get quick, visual inspiration from other counselors in the field. Don't forget to check out people's stories—I love how counselors will walk me through their ideas and implementation with video.

—Rebecca Atkins, school counselor in North Carolina

the American School Counseling Association unleashes a fun daily photo challenge to school counselors. Toward the end of the school year, counselors share favorite memories and ideas for summer self-care and ideas for the upcoming school year.

Many counselors who worry about what to write or saying the wrong thing enjoy collaborating on Instagram because they can connect with others with simply an image. A few phrases like "FAFSA Information Bulletin Board" or "third-grade projects" help counselors feel comfortable sharing without worrying about writing a whole paragraph.

New to Instagram? Sign up on your phone (it's a free mobile app on iOS and Android).

Get started by following these accounts:

- ASCA @weareasca

- Danielle Schultz @sch_counselor

- Natalie Spencer @nspencerphd

- Susan Spellman-Cann @sspellmancann

- Rebecca Atkins @counselorupblog

- Laura Ross @lrossschcnslr

- LittleMissCounselor @LittleMissCounselor

Key hashtags to follow include:

- #scchat

- #CounselorsFollowCounselors

- #SchoolCounselor

- #SchoolCounseling

- #CounselorsOfInstagram

- #SchoolCounselorLife

- #SchoolCounselorsRock

- #hscchat

- #mscchat

- #escchat

When considering using Instagram as a professional tool, be sure to read your district's guidelines about social media accounts. Some schools have a shared department account and a handful of people have access to post. Schools generally have a social media policy that normally includes not following students and not posting photos of students. In the past, many school districts were reluctant to jump on social media, but today they see the positive aspects of having a curated presence. It's always best to do your homework on the policies before you get started.

LINKEDIN

RECOMMENDED GRADE LEVEL	ELEMENTARY SCHOOL	MIDDLE SCHOOL	HIGH SCHOOL
LEVEL OF DIFFICULTY	EASY	MODERATE	A LITTLE MORE ADVANCED
COST	FREE	FREE TO USE PAY TO UPGRADE	FREE TRIAL PAY TO ACCESS

LinkedIn (LinkedIn.com) is often one of the first points of entry into using technology for a professional purpose. Starting in college, many young professionals set up an account when looking for an internship and first job. As a professional networking site, it's an accepted platform to highlight education, accomplishments (awards, publications, presentations), and work experience.

Signing up is free and easy. You simply input your first name, last name, email address, and a password of six or more characters. LinkedIn makes it easy for you to add your education, work experience, and accomplishments. Get started in making connections to your alumni group, connecting with colleagues, and following organizations you are interested in. You may also want to follow organizational leaders and role models who inspire you to see their updates in your LinkedIn news feed.

As a general rule of LinkedIn etiquette, you should make connections to people you actually know. If you want to connect with someone outside of your network, include a note explaining why or see if you have a mutual connection who can make an introduction. The number of people in your network isn't important. The quality of your connections is key.

Connect with groups, such as your college alumni group. Search on LinkedIn by your university name to find classmates. You can also connect with counselor organizations such as your state school counselor association and other state associations. You can also search "school counselor" to find active counselors on LinkedIn. This can be helpful if you want to connect with a counselor who has similar responsibilities or specialties. For example, if you are the counselor assigned to be the "anti-bullying specialist," it is helpful to connect with other counselors who also have this responsibility.

You can also make connections by sharing out articles on LinkedIn with comments and an open-ended question to spark discussion. Simply sharing articles is unlikely to result in high engagement. You can also write your own articles and share them on LinkedIn.

If you are a new professional or reentering the workforce, asking for recommendations from managers you worked for, classmates you partnered with on projects, or others who can speak to your skills can build up your profile. For example, let's say an FBI agent takes some time off of work after infiltrating the Miss United States pageant to prevent an attack on the event. She spends her time speaking at local events and teaching self-defense classes. When she is ready to rejoin the FBI, she asks for LinkedIn recommendations from her supervisor, colleagues, and from the women in the pageant. Miss Rhode Island's Cheryl Frasier gives Agent Gracie Hart a glowing recommendation for saving her life while bringing more humor to the pageant process. Having recommendations from supervisors, colleagues, and clients helps Agent Hart land the position of FBI director.

LinkedIn is not only a professional networking site but also a way for you to promote a positive, polished image of yourself as a professional.

LinkedIn is a great place to get started on having a professional online presence. Many hiring managers report that they search a potential candidate's name online to see what comes up. In schools, this is becoming a more common practice as well. Think of your online presence as the first impression others may have of you. LinkedIn is not only a professional networking site but also a way for you to promote a positive, polished image of yourself as a professional.

NOTES

GOOGLE DOCS

RECOMMENDED GRADE LEVEL	ELEMENTARY SCHOOL	MIDDLE SCHOOL	HIGH SCHOOL
LEVEL OF DIFFICULTY	EASY	MODERATE	A LITTLE MORE ADVANCED
COST	FREE	FREE TO USE PAY TO UPGRADE	FREE TRIAL PAY TO ACCESS

> Google Docs is my tech tool of choice when collaborating and supporting students as they apply to colleges, universities, careers, and trades. They begin their personal statements, their résumés, and their supplemental essays using the program. I can then add suggestions for editing to highlight the parts of their writing that will most appeal to the reader. This allows me, as their high school counselor, to not only check what they plan to send but to also debrief with students about professional expectations.
>
> —Alicia Oglesby, assistant director of college counseling,
> School Counselor of the Year (2017–2018),
> Bishop McNamara High School, Forestville, MD

Shortly after stone tablets, papyrus, and slate were created Google Docs debuted. Google Docs is a word processing application, capable of drafting, editing, and sharing texts and other simple documents (flyers, pamphlets, reports, etc.). Similar to other word processing programs such as Microsoft Word and Apple Pages, Google Docs creates rich documents. The service also offers auto-saving and archiving of previously saved versions, collaboration, and easy sharing of documents.

How do I get started? The only thing you need is an email to register for a Google Account (see "Getting Started With Google," page 42). From the Google Home Screen, you will access Google Drive. Google Drive can be accessed from App Launcher (the 9 dots in the upper right-hand corner or the home screen), going to drive.google.com. Once you're at the Google Drive screen, you'll see New in the upper left-hand corner. Click on the button and select Google Docs. You can also download and open the free app or go to docs.new or docs.google.com on a web browser.

You're ready to begin; users can select a new blank document or one from a series of templates; brochures, newsletters, consultation agreement, lesson plans, and much more can be found already formatted through Templates.

Using Google Docs is similar to other word processing applications. Users can write, insert tables and pictures (from their computer or URL or web search), check spelling and word count, and format the document for the appropriate purpose and stylistic preferences.

Google Docs also has a few distinct features. First, the document automatically saves to the web. You can stop writing on your work computer and pick up writing at home on a home computer or mobile device. If someone were to accidentally delete portions or the entirety of the document, selecting File, then Version History, or simply clicking on "All changes saved in Drive," located at the top of the screen, allows users to view and restore previous versions of the document. A copy of the document can be made simply by clicking on Make a copy. The document can be shared with colleagues to view, edit collaboratively, and/or provide comments on written work. The original owner of the document can set the editing rights.

One tool, Voice Typing, can be a great and useful adaptive tool for the educator on the go or students with a visual or motor impairment. Finally, the Explore button in the lower right-hand corner is like a research assistant, providing the ability to do a Google Search while writing a document, scan the document, and provide research suggestions (automatically citing it).

Counselors love to use Google Docs to write collaborative documents with colleagues and students, keep notes, and quickly draft brochures or other professional documents. The quick collaboration makes it useful for both students and educators, and the autosave and accessibility make the app nearly essential. As a tool of communication and expression, particularly with some of the Google Add-ons (page 52) tools, Google Docs is limited only by an internet connection and imagination.

NOTES

GOOGLE HANGOUTS

RECOMMENDED GRADE LEVEL	ELEMENTARY SCHOOL	MIDDLE SCHOOL	HIGH SCHOOL
LEVEL OF DIFFICULTY	EASY	MODERATE	A LITTLE MORE ADVANCED
COST	FREE	FREE TO USE PAY TO UPGRADE	FREE TRIAL PAY TO ACCESS

Google Hangouts is a communication service provided by Google. Through Hangouts, users can chat online and make video calls or phone calls, as well as collaborate and connect seamlessly across states with sharing screens, talking face to face, over the phone, or via messaging. A Wi-Fi connection can bridge some of the most distant connections. Counselors can connect with colleagues for virtual meetings or involve parents in meetings in a more personal way. Even distant cousins, nearly *Perfect Strangers*, could connect from places like Chicago to distant Mediterranean Islands, as if they were in the next room.

Hangouts lets you connect with colleagues in video chats. Virtual meetings can be set up by opening up a video call and sharing the link to participants' email or by attaching a link through a Google Calendar invite (see Google Calendar, page 62). Parents unable to attend a meeting can now join a video call with only a Wi-Fi connection and email. Through Google Hangouts you can make calls to parents via a smartphone app or computer and not have to share your phone number.

You will need a Google Account to get started (see "Getting Started With Google," page 42). From there you're ready to go; click on the app launcher in the upper right-hand corner of the Google Home Screen and click More. Hangouts will be located toward the bottom of the list. You can also type in the URL: hangouts.google.com. An app can be downloaded for both iOS and Android devices.

To make calls from Google Hangouts, you'll need to register your phone. Simply click on Phone Call (an image of a phone) and then New Conversation in the dialogue box. The dialogue box will ask you to "Enter name, email, or phone." Enter a phone number, even if it's your own. Google will now ask you to register your phone number. After entering your phone number, Google will text or call you with a verification code. Type in the code and you're ready to make calls. Video calls and chats via Hangouts need no additional registration other than a Google Account. The registered phone number with Google Hangouts allows users to add participants to a virtual meeting (a video call) when the participant can only participate via phone call. The use of video calls can promote accessibility to a remote meeting for participants who are deaf or hearing impaired. The use of screen sharing on video calls increases productivity and information sharing of a virtual meeting.

Other features include the ability to archive chats and adjust notification settings. You can also set privacy settings to limit who can contact you via Hangouts.

Google Hangouts is a great free service to increase connectivity with others. Networking (even across time zones) through video chats becomes easy with a simple calendar invite, and accessibility to (school) meetings can increase by opening up the traditional phone meeting to video chats with only a Wi-Fi connection. The ease and practical nature of the service makes us so happy we could do the Dance of Joy!

WEEBLY

RECOMMENDED GRADE LEVEL	ELEMENTARY SCHOOL	MIDDLE SCHOOL	HIGH SCHOOL
LEVEL OF DIFFICULTY	EASY	MODERATE	A LITTLE MORE ADVANCED
COST	FREE	FREE TO USE PAY TO UPGRADE	FREE TRIAL PAY TO ACCESS

Weebly is a website hosting platform. The service allows users to build quality websites with no coding experience. Weebly for Education offers their platform to use for FREE for educators and their students. The use of drag-and-drop features allows users to build blogs and websites quickly with the same effort it would take to make a PowerPoint presentation or pamphlet. Counselors and educators can create websites to share materials with students, host resources, stage virtual learning activities such as a flipped classroom, or brief a virtual space to educate students and families about the counseling program. Students can use the space (monitored by an adult) to develop near futuristic technical skills, use the sites as a blog or e-journal (reflecting on how historical figures have impacted their current relationships or academic plans), or develop school community pieces (such as a site for the school Battle of the Bands or their performance group—WYLD STALLYNS!)

Getting started is easy; just head to education.weebly.com. Users only need an email! Then you'll need to add a username and password. You're ready to begin! You can provide additional registration information or skip this step.

Weebly offers a demo video (only viewable through a flash player), and users can choose to begin building a website or create a classroom for students. When creating a classroom, users simply name the virtual classroom, which can hold up to 40 students. Students can be added manually (Weebly will even auto-generate a username for the students) or be uploaded en masse through a CSV file with first name, last name, username, and password. The teacher's dashboard can set the web pages to public or private. The classroom-only view will help protect student privacy. The teacher dashboard allows the educator to delete pages, if necessary, or simply view recent edits and changes on student pages.

Student website building and teacher website building use the same easy features. Editing can be done through the web browser on a computer or through the Weebly app. From the Build tab, titles and text can be changed by a simple click and typing. Features that can be dragged onto the pages include text boxes, galleries, and slideshows. Media can be added by dragging and uploading them onto the web page, such as YouTube videos, PDF files, audio files, and more. Images can be uploaded from a library, URL, or the large stock photo library from Weebly. Additional pages can be added through the Pages tab and edited using the same Build features. The sites themes including colors and fonts can be changed through the Themes tab.

The Setting feature allows users to change the title of the website or site address after the site is published. Users can also manage cookie notification through Settings and address the site's Search Engine Optimization (SEO). Additional editors and members to the site can also be added, as well as several premium features available for purchase. You can also unpublish the site from Settings.

The page can be built for either a desktop view or mobile view. The site will appear optimized to the viewer for either a desktop or mobile screen.

The ease of use with Weebly makes it perfect for family engagement, outreach, marketing, and communication, or an entry-point for website design. Counselors love the tool to promote programs and share resources; students love the site for a chance to make real digital artifacts. (Two students from San Dimas report the Tool is *excellent* and not bogus.) The sleek designs create a pleasing and professional look, while still allowing for a range of rich media to be supported on the site. Weebly for education can be used to create sites for individuals or organizations, create student sites, or build student portfolios. Website building has never been easier!

NOTES

_____

_____

_____

_____

_____

_____

_____

_____

_____

_____

_____

_____

_____

_____

_____

_____

_____

_____

_____

_____

APPY PIE

RECOMMENDED GRADE LEVEL	ELEMENTARY SCHOOL	MIDDLE SCHOOL	HIGH SCHOOL
LEVEL OF DIFFICULTY	EASY	MODERATE	A LITTLE MORE ADVANCED
COST	FREE	FREE TO USE PAY TO UPGRADE	FREE TRIAL PAY TO ACCESS

If, as an app developer, you have an idea of what you want your users to know and/or understand, you'll have a better sense of what you want the app to do.

Appy Pie is an app builder that allows users to make apps quickly with no coding experience. The app builder is easy to use with several customizable apps to choose from. Users simply drag-and-drop the features they want, and then publish. Apps can be created for Android and iOS, as well as other operating systems. Appy Pie allows a school counselor to make an app for the comprehensive counseling program to provide resources and information to parents. A student could make an app for the "Save Ferris" Bueller campaign to do outreach for an absent student having the day of his life in Chicago.

Getting started is easy. First, you simply name the app; no sign-in is needed. Once the app is named, you're ready to go. First, you'll be asked to select a category. There are dozens of categories to choose from! Entertainment, Education, Fitness, and Restaurants can be selected, but there are dozens of additional categories offered simply by clicking "View more categories." Next you'll be asked to Design the app. The layout of buttons and menus can be selected from several templates with features for each design customized to the type of app selected.

Once a layout has been selected, users can customize buttons, menus, and features using the My Features and Design Customization tabs. Each category has specific features already added. Buttons can be edited or removed by pressing on the pencil that appears when you hover over the button in the My Features menu; buttons can be moved by clicking and grabbing the dots that appear at the top of each button under the same menu.

Changes can be viewed and tested by the interactive virtual phone that appears to the right of the My Features menu. Twitter, Facebook, Google Drive, and other popular web-based services work without any noticeable bugs. Clicking on each button allows for the editing of text to change the title, description, or customization such as background images or colors. A counselor could make an app designed in the school colors, with tweets from the school district's Twitter account and information from tweets from a college board going directly to students or families. A student on his day off with his friends could directly upload to the app YouTube videos of "Danke Schoen" and "Twist and Shout" from Chicago's Von Steuben Day Parade or send push notifications for a crowd to start a flash mob and dance along.

Once the app has been formatted to the user's pleasure, you're ready to publish. Simply press Save and Continue and you're ready to go. Appy Pie will ask users to register. You can register with an email, Google, or Facebook account. Users will be prompted to, but do not need to, purchase a plan. Plans range in cost, with some costing up to several hundreds of dollars for an annual plan; the more expensive plan will publish apps to multiple platforms seamlessly.

For free plans, you will now have access to the Dashboard. The Dashboard will allow users to continue editing under Editor, view the Email Templates that can auto-generate email to users, and publish the app to friends, family members, or colleagues under Test App. The app is now ready to download through a URL and QR code onto Android devices. iOS devices can also download the app through QR code and URL but will also need to download a free PWA (progressive web app) to assist in navigation. Appy Pie will provide a guide for the easy download of its app under the Test App menu.

The secret to success with Appy Pie is one familiar to the seasoned educator. You must go into app building with a plan, just as you would when designing a sound curriculum. If, as an app developer, you have an idea of what you want your users to know and/or understand, you'll have a better sense of what you want the app to do. Appy Pie may require additional research or use of third-party apps or programs to find the right solution; but it remains an easy way to make quick functioning apps to suit most needs.

> What I like most about Appy Pie is how seamless its prototyping interface is. It's all drag-and-drop, and this makes it very easy to teach young budding app developers, especially those in elementary and middle school, how to wireframe and begin to bring their app concept to life.
>
> —Malavika Vivek, cofounder, Girls Make Apps

NOTES

_____

_____

_____

_____

_____

_____

_____

_____

_____

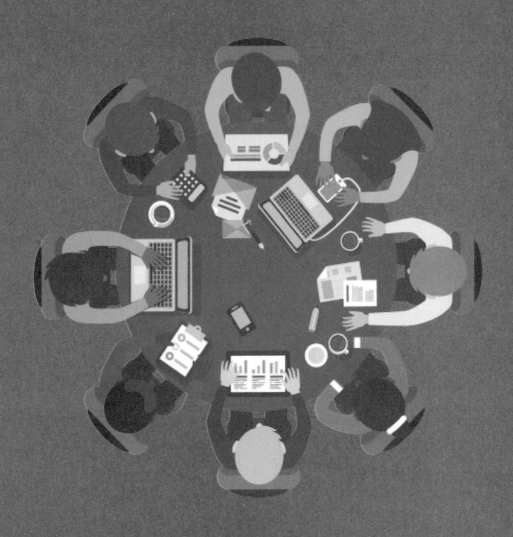

PART VI

RESOURCES

COMMON SENSE

RECOMMENDED GRADE LEVEL	ELEMENTARY SCHOOL	MIDDLE SCHOOL	HIGH SCHOOL
LEVEL OF DIFFICULTY	EASY	MODERATE	A LITTLE MORE ADVANCED
COST	FREE	FREE TO USE PAY TO UPGRADE	FREE TRIAL PAY TO ACCESS

Educators, especially school counselors and educational technology professionals, are in a unique position to address technology both proactively as part of a curriculum and, unfortunately, reactively after poor choices have been made. Administrators, fellow educators, families, and students turn to school counselors for support and information. However, technology changes at a rapid pace, and it's hard to keep up with the latest apps, social media challenges, internet crazes, and more.

Common Sense Media, commonsensemedia.org, empowers educators with unbiased, research-based tools to inform and guide students, families, and educational policy. As the leading independent nonprofit in the media and technology education arena, school counselors and administrators trust their high-quality curriculum, resources, and ratings and reviews of digital tools.

Common Sense Media offers free and engaging webinars and other types of professional development. You can read case studies from other schools and view a variety of short videos from their library. Many counselors use these videos to introduce a lesson, on morning announcements, and embed the videos into the school counselor website to add engaging, meaningful content.

The free downloadable posters, interactive content, lesson plans, and more address current challenges in our digital world. For example, check out the Deceptive Detective poster that teaches elementary school students how to spot deceptive news stories. The Legit-O-Meter poster addresses the same topic for older children. One of their most popular posters with school counselors is Oversharing: Think Before You Post. The second page ties content to the fun Flocabulary song with the same title.

There are great reminders for educators about dos and don'ts around social media use. While school counselors tend to be very well-versed in confidentiality practices, new platforms provide us with an opportunity to review policy and best practices. "Protecting Student Privacy on Social Media: Do's and Don'ts for Teachers" is a great reminder for educators.

The preamble of the ASCA Ethical Standards for School Counselors (2016) states, "All students have the right to: • Privacy that should be honored to the greatest extent possible, while balancing other competing interests (e.g., best interests of students, safety of others, parental rights) and adhering to laws, policies and ethical standards pertaining to confidentiality and disclosure in the school setting."

Rather than being the individual gatekeeper of students' privacy, counselors can point to guidelines in this resource. For example, did you know that student handwriting is considered identifying information? Simply covering a name but sharing out handwritten information can be a serious violation of privacy. Think of how embarrassing it can be if your student's note to you with photos of her cats in the same outfits, asking your advice about "Who wore it best?" were to become public, even if you covered the student's name!

The K–12 Digital Citizenship Curriculum (2018) "teaches students how to thrive in the digital age with free, research-backed lesson plans." It's customized by grade level: K–2, 3–5, 6–8, 9–12. You can filter lessons by content, such as Cyberbullying and Digital Drama, Digital Footprint & Reputation, Self-Image & Identity, and so on. These are all topics school counselors across the nation are covering on a regular basis, and having engaging, current, research-based curriculum that a counselor without a high level of expertise in technology can deliver is key to helping our students achieve a healthy relationship with technology.

Technology can be used as a tool to unlock a world of possibilities for a young person. However, as our youngest surfers begin to adopt habits online, an important priority of ours has to be not only keeping them safe but also teaching them to be masters in these skills so that they can grow to be accountable digital leaders. Especially as larger-scale data breaches and cyberattacks make headlines every day, we need to be learning, from the youngest of ages, how to best protect our identities online and reduce as much risk as possible. In doing so, we can make cybersecurity skills second nature (just like brushing teeth or locking cars) and foster the next generation of white-hat cyberdefenders who are working to prevent the next global cyberthreats.

—Kyla Guru, 16-year-old junior from Illinois.

The summer before her freshman year of high school, Kyla discovered her unique passion for cybersecurity, fascinated by the task of protecting our future technologies. With this discovery, she also learned that 90 percent of cyber-attacks on infrastructure were due to human error—a problem, she felt, future generations could not be burdened with. To combat this, Kyla founded Bits N' Bytes Cybersecurity (www.bitsnbytes.us.com), a nonprofit organization that now sustains 20+ national partnerships with school districts, corporations like ISACA and IBM, education platforms including Discovery Ed and TEDed, and U.S. representatives to increase dialogue for global cybersecurity and privacy issues and empower all users of the internet to be aware and educated online.

Cybersecurity and digital citizenship are topics counselors address on a regular basis with educators, families, and students. Everyone needs to know how to be responsible and safe online. Counselors don't have to know it all, but they do need to know where to look for reliable information on a regular basis. This old proverb holds true today: An ounce of prevention is worth a pound of cure.

NOTES

PINTEREST

RECOMMENDED GRADE LEVEL	ELEMENTARY SCHOOL	MIDDLE SCHOOL	HIGH SCHOOL
LEVEL OF DIFFICULTY	EASY	MODERATE	A LITTLE MORE ADVANCED
COST	FREE	FREE TO USE PAY TO UPGRADE	FREE TRIAL PAY TO ACCESS

Pinterest (pinterest.com) is an ever-growing compilation of ideas, projects, information, and inspiration. Its user-friendly interface displays small-scale images, videos, and GIFs with short descriptions that direct users to the site of origin for more information. Pinterest can be the best friend of any educator because it contains millions of creative ideas, successful counseling activities, educator blogs, and tools targeted to the unique needs of every professional in a K–12 setting.

If you are in need of a new activity to accompany a school counseling lesson, a different approach to work with a student, or office and/or classroom decor ideas to increase student comfort, Pinterest can be your go-to site. Simply search your need, and Pinterest will present thousands of ideas.

The ASCA (2006) position statement "The School Counselor and Equity for All Students" states that "School counselors recognize and distinguish individual and group differences and strive to equally value all students and groups. School counselors are advocates for the equitable treatment of all students in school and in the community." Counselors can find engaging and effective resources and ideas on Pinterest to meet the individual needs of their school.

Pinterest has its own language, which is quick to pick up. Pins are each of the small-scale images, GIFs, and videos. Pins serve as a hyperlink to the site the image originated from. If you have ever scrolled through a blog or magazine website, you may have noticed the small Pinterest logo under an article. Clicking it lets you share or pin the article for others in the Pinterest universe to see. An image usually accompanies an article, so when you pin it, the image shows as the hyperlink. Pinners are you and others who share, save, and pin on Pinterest.

Boards are where you save pins you want to reference again or save for later. You can create your own boards on your profile or when you select a pin. Pinning to a board is much like bookmarking a website. Your boards can have categories like individual counseling, group counseling, bulletin board ideas, counseling tools, and so on.

Follow is a function to see boards, pinners, and categories that most interest you. Following allows Pinterest to notify you of new pins from your favorite areas and helps suggest other pins and boards you may be interested in. If you become an avid pinner you may also get notified of pinners following you!

While Pinterest cannot be used without an account, a Pinterest account is free! You can sign up with an email or link to your Facebook or Google account:

1. When you open your account, Pinterest asks a few questions to suggest pins you may be interested in on your main search page. Pins will more align with your interests as you begin pinning.

2. Start scrolling through suggested interests or utilize the search bar for more specific topics.

3. The Explore tab on the menu bar also lets you search Pinterest by selected categories.

4. The Follow tab recommends boards and people who share your interests. The Follow tab is also where you can access people and boards you already follow.

5. Select your Profile tab to see your boards, followers, and favorite categories. This is where you can reference pins you saved.

6. Share pins with other pinners or social media friends through Messages. And see new pin notifications from your favorite boards.

You can link your Pinterest profile and boards to your social media page to share with others. For example, sharing a board for Growth Mindset quotes, books, and activities on your Facebook or Instagram allows others to see the pins! Create shared boards with colleagues or friends when working on projects, or even create a personalized vision board to help you stay focused on your personal and professional goals.

A favorite pinner of elementary school counselor materials is Susan Fuller's board: www.pinterest.com/eelementarysc

When I first began my career as a school counselor, we all relied on getting ideas from resource books we had to purchase. They were expensive: Some were great, and many were duds. Pinterest has been a game changer for educators. I have always loved how visual it is! It is a way for me to not only get great ideas that I can use as is or spin to meet my needs, but it

(Continued)

(Continued)

also is a way for me to easily share my found ideas with others. I have also linked my blog to my Pinterest page—a quick way to share my latest blog posts with a lot of people!

—Dr. Susan Fuller is a Pennsylvania urban elementary school counselor, author of the blog Entirely Elementary . . . School Counseling, an adjunct professor, and the recent past president of Lehigh Carbon School Counselor Association (LCSCA).

With over 300 million users, you are sure to find helpful tips and popular pinners who can help you take your school counseling program to the next level.

NOTES

_____

_____

_____

_____

_____

_____

_____

_____

_____

_____

_____

_____

_____

_____

_____

_____

_____

_____

_____

_____

_____

TEACHERS PAY TEACHERS

RECOMMENDED GRADE LEVEL	ELEMENTARY SCHOOL	MIDDLE SCHOOL	HIGH SCHOOL
LEVEL OF DIFFICULTY	EASY	MODERATE	A LITTLE MORE ADVANCED
COST	FREE	FREE TO USE PAY TO UPGRADE	FREE TRIAL PAY TO ACCESS

Teachers Pay Teachers (TpT) (teacherspayteachers.com) is an online catalog filled with resources for professionals in all educational capacities, with over three million original materials made by educators for educators. The TpT marketplace is free to access and search with confidence, knowing each custom resource was created with in-classroom expertise.

The TpT marketplace has an abundance of counselor activity tracking materials, printable school counseling lessons, and other downloadable resources, like fonts, spreadsheets, presentations, and images. You can find sample planners, documentation tools, and resources that support the unique needs of your students.

A good rule of thumb when considering purchasing an item or recreating it is to consider the amount of time it would take you to the create the resource.

Resources are made by a counselor who understands the needs of other counselors. Purchasing these materials is supporting a fellow school counselor who took the time to produce and share their ideas. Many resources are shared for free! A good rule of thumb when considering purchasing an item or recreating it is to consider the amount of time it would take you to develop the resource from scratch.

One of the best features of the resources is that because they are made by counselors, they intuitively understand the tedious and challenging tasks counselors must accomplish. For example, when a student is home sick or hospitalized for extended periods of time, there are resources to enhance communication between teachers and family and the homebound instructor. Also, counselors understand the need to be organized and efficient in the midst of a role filled with last-minute emergencies. Teachers Pay Teachers is filled with a variety of organizational resources to meet every counselor's unique needs.

You do not need to set up a profile to search the site. However, if you would like to download a free resource, make a purchase, or become a seller, you will need to register for an account, selecting one of three membership types: a free basic membership, a free basic seller account, or a premium seller account for an annual cost.

1. Create an account! This requires your necessary contact information, country, state, and your grade range of interest. For your grade range of interest, the site asks what age range you teach, but don't let this deter you; there are thousands of resources for a variety of educational professions including school counselors.

2. You will enter your account landing page where you can begin your search. Select the grades you would like to find resources in, see trending items, or filter your searches with the many options down the left side of the page.

3. As you begin scrolling through the millions of resources, you can add items to your wish list or follow sellers so that you get notifications when they upload new materials.

4. Found the resource or materials you needed? Add them to your cart and check out! Free resources can be downloaded immediately, ideal for the frugal counselor.

Teachers Pay Teachers has a function of requesting a resource through your school to be paid for with school funding. When you find materials that may qualify to be covered by school funding, select Request Resource above the option to add the item to your cart. You will be asked to complete a short form, which includes your school's name and administrators' information. Once the form is complete, you will also be able to see if anyone else from your school has requested the item and any other materials requested by your colleagues. This is a benefit to you and your school, because some downloadable resources can have additional licenses purchased at a lower price. Once your administrator registers and creates a school account with TpT, the school will receive money to spend on materials.

NOTES

YOUTUBE

RECOMMENDED GRADE LEVEL	ELEMENTARY SCHOOL	MIDDLE SCHOOL	HIGH SCHOOL
LEVEL OF DIFFICULTY	EASY	MODERATE	A LITTLE MORE ADVANCED
COST	FREE	FREE TO USE PAY TO UPGRADE	FREE TRIAL PAY TO ACCESS

YouTube is way more than a video-sharing platform! It's your go-to resource to learn new tech tools and a resource for counseling lessons. Many people find that watching a video tutorial is much more beneficial than reading a how-to for something they are learning. Trying to find a tutorial about creating surveys on Google Forms? Go to YouTube! Need to figure out how to create a graph from the data in your spreadsheet? Go to YouTube! Looking for school counseling clips that address conflict resolution for middle school students? Go to YouTube!

Amidst clips of Minecraft and kids playing with toys, you can find gems on YouTube, connecting students to content through multimedia that are both poignant and resonate in a way your words cannot. Someone out there put a lot of work into these videos, and I can support their achievement by sharing them at the same time helping my cause. Win-Win!

—Anhtu Conlon, school counselor, Texas

YouTube is a great tool to research tech-related topics for work. For example, if you wanted to conduct a needs assessment to guide your program goals and need to figure out the correct formulas to use, you can look up this information on YouTube. You can watch people's computer screens as they explain things, and you can mirror it on your own computer. Plus, you can rewatch videos as many times as you need to!

YouTube has a lot of accessibility features to meet the needs of all viewers. Closed captioning and subtitles in other languages allow all viewers to experience content. Students with visual impairments can use screen reader to listen to descriptions of what is happening on the screen. Users can also alter the features on their devices to enlarge the screen and change color brightness and contrast.

YouTube makes sharing information easy for content creators and accessible to users. Get started on creating video tutorials by thinking about the most common questions you are asked by families and teachers. "How do I upload grades?" "How do I access my child's report card?" "How do I add money to a lunch account?" Often the explanation for these questions requires a lengthy response if written. However, if you record your screen and explain how to do these things, a video tutorial will often require just a couple of minutes.

Creating the video tutorials to answer FAQs saves time in responding individually and also is very beneficial to users. Viewers feel like they are receiving a personalized response from us because it contains the familiar voice of their school counselor (and counselors can include themselves in the video!) and we personalized content to our community. Get started on making videos by downloading the screen recording Chrome extension Screencastify. You can make videos that don't exceed 10 minutes on the free version, which is more than enough time for video tutorials. We recommend keeping the video tutorials under 3 minutes.

Last, like many other educators, counselors face program budget cuts and outdated resources. Did we really want to spend our limited pennies on outdated VHS-based programs? No! Search YouTube for engaging video clips of modern TV shows and current cartoons that introduced topics such as conflict. Search for videos that introduce skills such as active listening, using I-messages, and more. Rather than relying upon a set lesson from a distributor, customize content to meet the unique needs of your student population.

YouTube is a current resource to find videos about many career pathways. The ASCA position statement "The School Counselor and Career Development" states, "School counselors recognize that each student, regardless of background, possesses unique interests, abilities and goals, which will lead to future opportunities. Collaborating with students, families, educational staff and the community, the school counselor works to ensure all students select a postsecondary path to productive citizenry (e.g., military, career technical certificate or two-/four-year degree program) appropriate for the student" (ASCA, 2017a). Counselors address this by incorporating videos about careers, pathways, and insights into the field into classroom lessons and career presentations with families.

Getting started on YouTube is easy and free. Rather than jumping right in, create a few playlists to organize videos you save. We got started by creating playlists based on large group lesson topics (conflict resolution, digital citizenship, study skills, etc.). Search on YouTube for your favorite TED Talks, Kid President videos, or other videos that you can imagine using in a lesson. We also created playlists called *Teacher Tutorials* and *Family FAQ* to organize the content we created specifically for these audiences. Based on your student population, you may want to customize content into a playlist. For example, at the high school level, you can create a playlist about financial aid, writing a college essay, or information about joining the military. Encourage your students (and families) to subscribe to this playlist so that they get the latest updates via an automatic alert from YouTube and you don't have to send an email each time you upload new content.

SAFESHARE

RECOMMENDED GRADE LEVEL	ELEMENTARY SCHOOL	MIDDLE SCHOOL	HIGH SCHOOL
LEVEL OF DIFFICULTY	EASY	MODERATE	A LITTLE MORE ADVANCED
COST	FREE	FREE TO USE PAY TO UPGRADE	FREE TRIAL PAY TO ACCESS

SafeShare provides the counselor with a platform to safely share this YouTube clip without worries that comments or suggested videos with spoofs of this episode will detract from the seriousness of the message.

Do you have a limited budget? Do you want modern, meaningful content for lessons? Do you find that by the time you purchase any curriculum with DVDs, the out-of-date fashion distracts students from the lessons?

You've probably looked up YouTube videos to incorporate in lessons but worry about inappropriate comments that appear underneath a great clip. Advertisements that play before or in the middle of a clip take away from valuable time with your audience. A "suggested" next video that autoplays can quickly transform an engaging hook to an embarrassing nightmare.

If any of this sounds familiar, there is a simple, free solution in SafeShare (safeshare .tv). Simply copy the URL of the YouTube or Vimeo video and paste it into the bar and select the arrow to create your SafeShare video.

You'll be prompted to sign up for an account (your email and add a password). From there, you can select your video and clip it (both start and end) to show the part you select. The new SafeShare link allows you to safely share videos with just a blank screen in the background. There are no ads, no suggested videos, no comments, and only YOUR video will play.

For example, a school counselor may want to introduce the topic of hidden dangers of caffeine pills using a clip of Jessie Spano's moving performance on *Saved by the Bell*, screeching, "I'm so excited...I'm so exciteeeed!...I'm so...SCARED!" SafeShare provides the counselor with a platform to safely share this YouTube clip without worries that comments or suggested videos with spoofs of this episode will detract from the seriousness of the message.

The SafeShare link never expires. Some schools block YouTube or Vimeo, but you can ask your IT department to contact SafeShare. Often schools are thrilled to find that educators can make use of free content to enhance lessons in a safe way.

The free account is ideal for most counselors, because they are teaching a smaller number of lessons using videos compared to other educators. With the free version, you can adjust the video's range and create up to 20 SafeViews. You can also create playlists and share your lists with others. This is an especially helpful feature to create customized helpful video resources differentiated by grade level of students, students' needs, and collaborating to share video resources with counselor colleagues.

NOTES

_____

_____

_____

_____

_____

_____

_____

_____

_____

_____

_____

_____

_____

_____

_____

_____

_____

_____

_____

_____

_____

_____

_____

_____

QUIZLET

RECOMMENDED GRADE LEVEL	ELEMENTARY SCHOOL	MIDDLE SCHOOL	HIGH SCHOOL
LEVEL OF DIFFICULTY	EASY	MODERATE	A LITTLE MORE ADVANCED
COST	FREE	FREE TO USE PAY TO UPGRADE	FREE TRIAL PAY TO ACCESS

One of the most common requests educators get from families is study skills support for students. Both families and teachers appreciate strategies that are transferable to other subject areas and incorporated into a student's toolbox of skills. It's empowering for students to learn skills and tools to be successful across academic subjects.

Quizlet (quizlet.com) is a fantastic tech tool that takes a familiar strategy of studying with paper flashcards then digitizes and enhances it. Students can create their own digital flashcards and study on the go from their devices.

It's empowering for students to learn skills and tools to be successful across academic subjects.

Students can download the free Quizlet app and study flashcards from their smartphone. They can "star" cards they want to study separately for more focused review. Having the cards on their smartphone allows students to study on the fly and for short or long sessions. It's a great resource for busy families!

Signing up is free and easy. You'll need your email address and to create a username and password. You can search the database of free cards to see if there are any sets that cover your topic or you can create your own. Creating cards is simple; enter the term and the definition on the designated lines.

You can also upload an entire set of cards by copying and pasting data from a document or spreadsheet. This is a really useful tool if you have a study skills group. Students can work on a shared document to create a list of terms and definitions, and you can upload them to your account or they can upload the entire set to their accounts.

Quizlet offers more than flashcards. The Spell feature is great practice for spelling exams. Students type the word that is read to them. The Match game is a fun way to connect terms and definitions. The Test is a great review, and the Gravity game is a speed test where players protect the planets from incoming asteroids.

Educators use Quizlet in study groups and share it with students and families as an accessible technology tool that enhances learning and retention of information. School counselors are also using Quizlet to search for study cards to support their own learning in preparation for national or state exams. It's a versatile resource!

STITCHER

RECOMMENDED GRADE LEVEL	ELEMENTARY SCHOOL	MIDDLE SCHOOL	HIGH SCHOOL
LEVEL OF DIFFICULTY	EASY	MODERATE	A LITTLE MORE ADVANCED
COST	FREE	FREE TO USE PAY TO UPGRADE	FREE TRIAL PAY TO ACCESS

Stitcher is a streaming audio service that provides podcasts on demand from a mobile listening device or web browser. Podcasts are streaming news, sports, and talk radio and in many cases free high-quality professional development. Podcasts allow users to potentially have a powerful learning experience while doing things such as using their hands for things like work or driving or remain in more comfortable clothing such as sweats or a snuggy without a need to change. Stitcher is one of the premiere services for podcasts with an extensive and growing library.

Getting started is easy; you can provide an email or use your Facebook or Google account. Stitcher will ask to access your media library if you're using an Apple Device and to access your current location; neither is necessary to use the service.

Once registered, Stitcher will ask users to select shows based off of topics—News & Current Events, Comedy, Society & Culture, and more—or by popularity. A curated list of podcasts is now available on My Front Page, also available when you click on Listen on www.stitcher.com on your desktop. You can create a customized playlist of favorite podcasts. Stitcher will also recommend podcasts and shows based off of your listening history. Selected podcasts will also share with you what other Listeners Also Liked to expand the listeners' library. Premium content allows users to listen ad-free; there is additional exclusive content like Stitcher Originals, Bonus Episodes, and Comedy Albums for a fee.

In addition to the rich digital professional development, school counselors can use podcasts from services like Stitcher to provide valuable content to lessons. Compelling stories of *This American Life* or a TED Talk can frame a lesson or group or expand on content. Most content is easy to share via a link or email or even added to a Livebinder.

The ease of use, portability, and breadth and diversity of content makes a diet of podcasts necessary for any educator on the go. Stitchers' deep library and accessibility across platforms makes it one of the premier platforms for your podcast fix.

The Unofficial/Nonscientific Facebook Survey of Favorite Podcasts

We scoured the internet for minutes, possibly even a half hour, to see the favorite podcasts of educational Facebook groups. We noted the most popular responses when someone asked, "What are your favorite podcasts?" and then listed them here.

- *10 Minute Teacher*
- *Angela Watson's Truth for Teachers*
- *ASCA Podcast*
- *Code Switch*
- *Cult of Pedagogy*
- *Cutting Edge School Counseling*
- *edSurge On Air*
- *Getting In: Your College Admissions Companion*
- *Happier With Gretchen Rubin*
- *Harvard EdCast*
- *Hatching Results*
- *Lift Every Voice*
- *Stuff Mom Never Told You*
- *TED Talks Education*
- *The Social Work Podcast*
- *This American Life*

NOTES

_____

_____

_____

_____

_____

_____

_____

_____

_____

_____

_____

_____

_____

_____

GOOGLE FOR EDUCATION

RECOMMENDED GRADE LEVEL	ELEMENTARY SCHOOL	MIDDLE SCHOOL	HIGH SCHOOL
LEVEL OF DIFFICULTY	EASY	MODERATE	A LITTLE MORE ADVANCED
COST	FREE	FREE TO USE PAY TO UPGRADE	FREE TRIAL PAY TO ACCESS

You have arrived! Google for Education is the landing page for all the Google products that could be useful for educators, both the free and paid services. The range of services is comprehensive, spanning, and rapidly growing.

Starting on the landing page, you'll see six tabs across the top: Products; Teaching Resources; Computer Science; Training & Support; Giving; and The Latest. Each area has diverse services and products listed with many services interwoven.

Under the Products tab, K12 Solutions provides a list of the G Suite for Education core services, which are the bundle of intelligent apps designed by Google. You can sign up for a Gmail for FREE and access the many different Google services for FREE. G Suite Enterprise for Education is Google's fee-for-service or business services, including some that have features different from the free versions.

The K12 Solutions services also offer Classroom. Google Classroom is a great way to post, share, and receive assignments, increase communication, and promote access to educational materials from everywhere; but this service is only available for G Suite users.

K12 digital tools have some of the best features from Google for Education, including:

1. **Science Journal** is an app by Google that is a digital science journal that allows students to use their mobile device to record scientific notes, take photos, and use the phone's built-in sensors (lights, sound, motion, and more). Students can record observations and insights and create new experiments.

2. **Be Internet Awesome (BIA)** is a digital citizenship curriculum by Google for third through eighth grade, with aspects of the curriculum relevant for any grade level. The curriculum addresses issues of privacy and cybersecurity while talking about concepts such as kindness and conflict resolution in virtual spaces.

   You may be asking: *Who is best suited to teach the BIA curriculum?* As presented under "Frequently asked questions" in the Educator's Guide (Google, 2018):

   Do I need special training to complete this, or be a special kind of teacher?

   - First: Any K–12 teacher can teach this curriculum to their students. No extra training is required.

   - Second: Every teacher is special. :)

3. **Search Education** is the hidden curricular gem of Google that provides students of all ages with standards-driven language, tools, and resources to get the most out of web-based searches.

4. **Cultural Institute** shares the full breadth of Google Arts and Culture. Galleries, museums, historic events or locations, and much more are showcased here. This serves as a premiere showcase of visual mediums and human experiences.

5. **Google Scholar** is the Google Search feature for scholarly research. Google Scholar allows users to search for articles, abstracts, theses, court opinions, and books across disciplines.

6. **Google Earth Education** houses all Google Geo tools: Google Earth, My Maps, Tour Builder, Street View, Google Earth Engine, and Geo VR. Each of the services can help students experience distant lands, traveling along historic routes and paths, or observe and analyze Earth in unprecedented ways.

7. **Google Expeditions** is another K–12 service highlighted, able to use many of the same features of Google Earth Education in innovative and inspirational ways. Read more on page 31.

8. **IT Guide** has helpful information on safety and privacy and on Reference Districts across the United States, if you'd like to contact someone nearby on how they're using some of the services.

Higher Ed Solutions has valuable information for educators at any level. Valuable independent computer science learning activities for advanced secondary students can be found here. There is information on grant funding for educators and scholarship information for students. The most important resource is the research for uncovering obstacles toward computing careers. The research helps all those working support students in the twenty-first century (especially, underrepresented groups like women, students of color, and rural students). There is information to recognize and eliminate bias and tools to understand and navigate the many different systemic and structural barriers.

Computer Science provides the wealth of trainings and resources to support students and educators develop the technical skills to flourish. The resources for educators include the previously mentioned grants and research, as well as curriculum to introduce and explore concepts in computational thinking.

The resources for Google for Education are robust and ever growing. For educators looking to explore the vast world of instructional technology for themselves and twenty-first century skills for their students, there are a few "one-stop shops," and Google for Education is one of them. With most services on the site being FREE, Google for Education is a great place to explore to get the most out of the future of learning.

NOTES

_____

_____

_____

_____

_____

_____

NYTVR (NEW YORK TIMES VIRTUAL REALITY)

RECOMMENDED GRADE LEVEL	ELEMENTARY SCHOOL	MIDDLE SCHOOL	HIGH SCHOOL
LEVEL OF DIFFICULTY	EASY	MODERATE	A LITTLE MORE ADVANCED
COST	FREE	FREE TO USE PAY TO UPGRADE	FREE TRIAL PAY TO ACCESS

NYTVR or New York Times Virtual Reality is the virtual reality edition of the iconic newspaper. NYTVR provides captivating streaming 3-D videos able to be watched using a cellphone through a cardboard viewer or simply by turning the phone sideways. Through the phone, users can dive into stories from the pages of the *New York Times*, in the same quality and compelling nature of the Sunday edition.

The content of the *New York Times* has been and continues to be used in classrooms to explore relevant and current topics. While the writing has been used to elevate reading for students, the immersive virtual reality stories help users be enveloped into the text of the *New York Times* featured stories.

Unlike a growing segment of the *New York Times* print content, NYTVR and its content remains free. Getting started is as simple as downloading the free app for iOS or Android devices. The app is also available for free on Samsung VR. Once downloaded, you're ready to begin.

Similar to the *New York Times* leading podcast *The Daily*, NYTVR also produces the virtual reality The Daily 360. Daily videos are posted, sharing the *Times*'s compelling journalism in human interest, culture, and arts and humanities stories.

After Puerto Rico was devastated by a hurricane and the aftermath rippled throughout the lives of students and families across the island, it was impossible not to be moved with compassion and sadness. As the island began steps toward repair, stories of students and schools in harrowing conditions arose, and as our country mourned losses, students relocated to new states and communities. NYTVR's immersive piece *Dark Island* would be the best illustration of how school counselors and other educators could use this twenty-first-century tool, an engaging narrative from the premier storytelling of the *New York Times*, to serve as a medium to build empathy or provide a cultural foundation for an event of national significance.

NYTVR provides a great entry into virtual reality and a model for twenty-first-century storytelling. The price point of FREE and prevalence of mobile devices allow students to access the rich narratives and explore deeply the distant land and lives intimately.

CLOSING

This is a remix! Found on the B-side of most hip-hop singles of the '90s, the rise of the remix was one of the biggest pop culture changes in the twentieth century. Sampling, looping, mash-ups, and synthetic beats permeated the streets and art-house scene to reinvent and reimagine popular music. Just as it was fun and fresh to see Michael J. Fox sing the '50s classic "Johnny B. Goode," now the best parts of the '80s and '90s have been remixed and reimagined as Netflix Originals, Super Bowl commercials, and Nicki Minaj singles. The remix of the best parts of counseling and education are now being realized with the rich incorporation of technology.

- A MASH-UP of Google Calendar, YouCanBook.me and IFTTT can produce a Use of Time tracker to better analyze a comprehensive school counseling program's design and optimize performance.

- A LOOP of scheduled Tweets from TweetDeck or Buffer provides an ongoing conversation with students, parents, and other influencers to communicate, advocate, and connect to a school counseling program.

- A SAMPLING of the voices of leading professionals from the field through podcasts such as *Hatching Results* or *Cutting Edge School Counseling,* or Facebook Groups such as Caught in the Middle School Counselors or Professional School Counselors of Color, can provide clarity and confidence in a profession that often has moments of uncertainty.

Still, it's not the adding of an electronic drumbeat that makes a new song; rather, it's the infusion of technology to fundamentally shift and invigorate the familiar that draws us to remixes and revivals. Just as a brief trip to a high school prom in a DeLorean in the '80s could reshape your current world, the use of the Tech Tools can be used to reshape contemporary approaches of education and school counseling.

Through the course of the book, we hope you, the reader, have been exposed to a range of Tech Tools. Ideally, the goal was to provide apps, websites, and services that would help streamline the routine parts of the work and ease the complexity of some of the challenging aspects of your job. The use of social media, automation, artificial intelligence, and algorithmic processes has been neatly packaged between these pages to be more accessible than a computer science text book or three-credit course.

As highlighted throughout the book, the better the functions of the Tech Tools are understood, the deeper and broader the tools can be applied. Similarly, the use of the process known as *Design Thinking* can help school counselors and other users get more out of their Tech Tools. If a school counselor, or other educator, takes the time to observe and explore the Tech Tools and how the tools interact both with users and other systems, the educators will likely start to understand the elements and principles of Design Thinking.

The most exciting part is the application of Design Thinking. If school counselors better understand the principles of Design Thinking, they will be better equipped to help their students navigate the twenty-first century and build solutions to mediate problems and accomplish goals. The most exciting secret is one hinted at through the book. The use and strange familiarity of the application of the various new Tech Tools is at the heart of why school counselors were chosen for the focus of the book.

The thought process of Design Thinking is closely analogous to the systematic design and approach of the Comprehensive School Counseling System. The more counselors understand both the narrow and broad uses of comprehensive school counseling programs to improve their practice and enrich the lives of the students, the better school counselors will understand how to incorporate and apply a range of Tech Tools (including those yet to be invented). Better, the more counselors are able to understand the principles of Design Thinking, the more the counselor will be able to design, remix, and reimage the dimensions of practice, school counseling programs, and schools to meet ever-changing student needs.

Design Thinking is a human-centered process of identifying challenges and goals through the gathering of information to generate ideas (ideate) and build and refine strategies and solutions. The approach can be seen as a marrying of critical thinking and creativity highlighting skills such as empathy, collaboration, persistence, and curiosity.

Principles of Design Thinking

- **Empathy**—monitor, observe, and listen to connect
- **Define**—shift perspectives, clarity, and focus to key topics
- **Ideate**—through curiosity and imagination, brainstorm possibilities and potential solutions
- **Prototype**—implement the plans and approaches you've created, continue to reimagine them to new strategies
- **Evaluate**—assess and evaluate each new plan or approach: soliciting feedback, making observations, and shifting perspectives

---

Empathy is where designers build connections through questioning and observation to better understand their clients, the problems, and needs. School counselors are familiar with the practice of connecting with students and the school community through individual counseling, use of needs assessments, and feedback from the advisory boards. Many of the themes and goals for counseling programs to guide in their design efforts are anchored in foundation aspects of a comprehensive school counseling program.

- *Tech tools to help Empathize*: Flipgrid can explore thought and introspection in personal ways while broadening participation in and distribution of collective voices. Padlet makes a great introduction to learn to build student narrative or identify themes of student experience or school culture.

Define is where designers, through reflection, detect patterns or themes. The designers may detect patterns by narrowing the problem or highlighting specific points while they work toward a solution. Through use of program goals, school counselors narrow the focus of their program and through the use of the mindsets and behaviors drill down standards and goals to individual student competencies.

- *Tech tools to help Define*: Use Google Forms to generate feedback that can be quickly aggregated, analyzed, or distilled. Canva is an eye-capturing infographic that could best capture and communicate the goals.

Ideate is the open and rapid generation of ideas, best achieved by nonjudgmentally embracing the designer's creativity while guided from information gathered earlier in the process. School counselors are best able to generate solutions and ideas through consultation and the support of supervision, while relying on the key theme of collaboration.

- *Tech Tools to help Ideate*: Facebook, Pinterest, and Twitter are great for crowdsourcing ideas and soliciting quick feedback. Tools like Buffer allow a user to reach out to all at once in minutes.

Prototype is where the designer builds and/or implements a product or work about a selected idea. Prototypes have many purposes: to engage others in conversation or to communicate an idea or concept, further break down a problem as you work toward a solution, and continue to foster new ideas and directions. Counselors build prototypes most often in their Core Curriculum, whether in an action plan or lesson plans.

- *Tech Tools to help Prototype:* Nearpod offers counselors the opportunity to customize lessons with embedded feedback tools. PlayPosit is a platform to "flip" the video-based lessons counselors create and embed reflective questions and to make learning accessible to all students.

Evaluation lets the designer actively measure and assess the product or work. This part of the process is interwoven with the prototype phase. The school counselor's use of assessment to measure students' meeting competencies and measures of accountability, such as result reports and program assessment, drive the refinement of aspects of a program and generate new ideas. The use of ongoing collaboration in the evaluation process, such as the reviewing of the data and being guided by feedback from the advisory board, shows the cyclical nature of the design process in a comprehensive school counseling program.

- *Tech Tools to help Evaluate*: Google Sheets is fantastic for storing, sharing, and analyzing data. Kahoot is an engaging tool for measuring student learning in lessons and instruction.

The use of Design Thinking Principles—**Empathy, Define, Ideate, Prototype,** and **Evaluate**—is the key approach in getting most out of the Tech Tools, remixing them, and repurposing the many tools to suit your every need. The same principles can be used to reexamine and remix your school counseling practice and service to students.

The use of Tech Tools featured in this book will enhance productivity, streamline communication, and connect readers to a range of resources yet to be discovered. The adoption of the Tech Tools as instruments of experimentation and exploration will empower the reader with the resources needed to connect themselves and their students to the future.

This is a remix.

NOTES

_____

_____

_____

_____

_____

_____

_____

_____

_____

_____

_____

_____

_____

_____

_____

_____

_____

_____

_____

_____

_____

_____

REFERENCES

American School Counselor Association. (1974). *The school counselor and confidentiality.* Alexandria, VA: Author. Retrieved from http://www.schoolcounselor.org/asca/media/asca/PositionStatements/PS_Confidentiality.pdf

American School Counselor Association. (1988). *The school counselor and comprehensive school counseling programs.* Alexandria, VA: Author. Retrieved from http://www.schoolcounselor.org/asca/media/asca/PositionStatements/PS_ComprehensivePrograms.pdf

American School Counselor Association. (2000). *The school counselor and student safety and the use of technology.* Alexandria, VA: Author. Retrieved from http://www.schoolcounselor.org/asca/media/asca/PositionStatements/PS_Technology.pdf

American School Counselor Association. (2006). *The school counselor and equity for all students.* Alexandria, VA: Author. Retrieved from http://www.schoolcounselor.org/asca/media/asca/PositionStatements/PS_Equity.pdf

American School Counselor Association. (2012). *ASCA school counselor competencies.* Alexandria, VA: Author. Retrieved from http://www.schoolcounselor.org/asca/media/asca/home/SCCompetencies.pdf

American School Counselor Association. (2014). *Mindsets and behaviors for student success.* Alexandria, VA: Author. Retrieved from http://www.schoolcounselor.org/asca/media/asca/home/MindsetsBehaviors.pdf

American School Counselor Association. (2016). *ASCA ethical standards for school counselors.* Alexandria, VA: Author. Retrieved from http://www.schoolcounselor.org/asca/media/asca/Ethics/EthicalStandards2016.pdf

American School Counselor Association. (2017a). *The school counselor and career development.* Alexandria, VA: Author. Retrieved from http://www.schoolcounselor.org/asca/media/asca/PositionStatements/PS_CareerDevelopment.pdf

American School Counselor Association. (2017b). *The school counselor and virtual school counseling.* Alexandria, VA: Author. Retrieved from http://www.schoolcounselor.org/asca/media/asca/PositionStatements/PS_Virtual.pdf

American School Counselor Association. (2018). *The school counselor and career and technical education.* Alexandria, VA: Author. Retrieved from http://www.schoolcounselor.org/asca/media/asca/PositionStatements/PS_CTE.pdf

American School Counselor Association. (n.d.a). *Career conversation starters.* Alexandria, VA: Author. Retrieved from http://www.schoolcounselor.org/asca/media/asca/Publications/CareerConversationStarters.pdf

American School Counselor Association. (n.d.b). *High school career conversation starters.* Alexandria, VA: Author. Retrieved from http://www.schoolcounselor.org/asca/media/asca/Publications/HSCareerConversations.pdf

Common Sense. (2018). Digital citizenship. Retrieved from https://www.commonsense.org/education/digital-citizenship

Google. (2018). *Be internet awesome.* Retrieved from https://beinternetawesome.withgoogle.com/en_us/educators

Statista. (2018, January). Number of Facebook users by age in the U.S. as of January 2018 (in millions). Retrieved from https://www.statista.com/statistics/398136/us-facebook-user-age-groups/

United States Census Bureau. (n.d.). U.S. and world population clock. Retrieved from https://www.census.gov/popclock/

Zemeckis, R. (Producer and Director). (1985). *Back to the future* [Motion picture]. Universal City, CA: Universal Pictures.

INDEX

A SAGE Publishing Company

Helping educators make the greatest impact

CORWIN HAS ONE MISSION: to enhance education through intentional professional learning.

We build long-term relationships with our authors, educators, clients, and associations who partner with us to develop and continuously improve the best evidence-based practices that establish and support lifelong learning.

Solutions YOU WANT | Experts YOU TRUST | Results YOU NEED

EVENTS

>>> **INSTITUTES**

Corwin Institutes provide large regional events where educators collaborate with peers and learn from industry experts. Prepare to be recharged and motivated!

corwin.com/institutes

ON-SITE PD

>>> **ON-SITE PROFESSIONAL LEARNING**

Corwin on-site PD is delivered through high-energy keynotes, practical workshops, and custom coaching services designed to support knowledge development and implementation.

corwin.com/pd

>>> **PROFESSIONAL DEVELOPMENT RESOURCE CENTER**

The PD Resource Center provides school and district PD facilitators with the tools and resources needed to deliver effective PD.

corwin.com/pdrc

ONLINE

>>> **ADVANCE**

Designed for K–12 teachers, Advance offers a range of online learning options that can qualify for graduate-level credit and apply toward license renewal.

corwin.com/advance

Contact a PD Advisor at (800) 831-6640 or visit www.corwin.com for more information